TULIP QUILT

by
Eleanor Burns

For Mother

ISBN 0-922705-22-4

Copyright © 1991 by Eleanor Burns

First Printing March, 1991

Design and Layout - Quilt in a Day Art Dept.

Photography - Wayne Norton

Published by *Quilt in a Day*®

Quilt in a Day, Inc., 1955 Diamond Street, San Marcos, CA 92069

Printed in the United States of America

Table of Contents

As faithful as a true friend, the tulips popped their colorful heads above the ground every spring in Pennsylvania. I was only three when we lived on the old Wise farm in Harmony, but I still remember the tulips Mother and my sister, Kathy, planted along the fence. Perhaps the memory is so vivid because I was terrified of the cows just a step beyond. Spring was a sweet wonderland when we gathered armfuls of fresh tulips and bright daffodils.

When I was four, we moved to the house on Grandview Avenue that remained our roots until 1988. As soon as the packing crates were tossed, Mother taught me how to plant the bulbs along the stone wall -- tulips, daffodils, crocus, and hyacinth. We nurtured them, and, spring after spring, they miraculously graced our wall with their slender, colorful stature. Their presence was welcomed....the end of winter, a perfect hiding place for colorful Easter eggs, a backdrop for our neighborhood circus.

The whisper of a sweet fragrance in spring still reminds me of my mother, lovingly cutting tulips and wrapping their ends in wax paper for me to present to my favorite teacher. Mother nurtured and loved me, as we did the flowers. But then, isn't a mother's love for her child like the colors of the tulips: as pure as white, soft as pink, true blue, the yellow sunshine, and a sprinkling of purple passion.

The tulip quilt was first introduced in the January, 1989, issue of Craft Magazine with instructions for a double bed size quilt only. Because of its popularity, you can now make a tulip quilt in every size.

May the tulip quilt you create be as fresh and colorful as a mother's love.

Eleanor Burns

Eleanor Burns

The Tulip Block

The nine-patch tulip block is an easy one to make. The tip of the tulip is made with a "log cabin" method. The pieced squares for the tulip and leaves are sewn with quick grid marking and sewing techniques, and then squared up to match the size of the other pieces. The stem is topstitched to a background square.

Color Selection: Create a Garden

Select tulip fabrics in traditional reds, yellows, purples, oranges, or any color you choose from nature. Select leaf and stem fabrics in traditional hues of greens or blue/greens. Be wild and daring and make it bright blue, or any color you choose!

However, the value or darkness of the tulip color should be equal to or greater than the value of the leaves and stems to make the tulip stand out in the patchwork.

If you select a pastel color for the tulip, consider using a dark background fabric.

To avoid dull and boring quilts, remember to mix the scales of your prints as large scale prints, small scale prints, and ones that look like solids from a distance. Directional prints should not be used.

Multicolored Tulip Garden Variation

Make a refreshing tulip garden with flowers of many different fabrics and colors. Purchase several 1/3 yard pieces for the tulips and leaves. In addition, follow the Yardage Charts to help you with your estimates.

Set tulip blocks of the same color in diagonal rows, or across the rows on larger quilts.

Scrap Tulip Block

You can use scraps for variety. For each scrap flower block, you need:

Tip of Flower

(1) 2 3/8" square medium flower tip fabric

Flower

(1) 4" square dark flower fabric

(1) 4 1/2" square dark flower fabric

Leaves

(1) 4 1/2" square leaf fabric

Stem

(1) 1 1/2" x 6" stem fabric

Light Background

(1) 4 1/2" x 9" light

(3) 4" squares light

(1) 2 3/8" x 7 1/2" light

Follow the Yardage and Cutting Charts for the number of blocks you need for your particular quilt. Help coordinate the scrap flowers and leaves by using the same light background fabric in all the blocks. Refer to your Yardage Chart requirements for the light background, borders, and optional setting choices of solid squares or lattice and cornerstones.

Fabric Selection

"Fall in love" with one fabric, as a multicolored fabric, a larged scaled fabric, a stripe, or a motif. Once that fabric is selected, decide on the most appropriate placement for that fabric in either the tulip block or one of the two setting choices, and build the other fabrics around it.

The number of tulip blocks differs between the two settings.

1. Tulip with Solid Squares - Easy Design

A large scaled floral print is most appropriate for the solid squares. To avoid a "busy look" that detracts from the large floral, select fabrics that appear solid from a distance for the tulip and leaves.

"Floating" Tulips Variation

Use the same background fabric for the solid square as in the tulip block.

2. Tulip with Lattice and Cornerstones - Advanced Design

Any fabric of medium value can be used for the lattice. However, a striped fabric is perfect. If you wish to use a stripe, look for designs 2" wide plus 1/4" on each side for seam allowance. The stripes are cut lengthwise with the grain. Depending on the number of repeats of a 2 1/2" wide cut, you need additional yardage. See page 49 for more information.

To get maximum use from a fabric with several striped designs, a second stripe design 2 3/8" wide can be used for the flower tip. Coordinating fabrics generally manufactured to compliment the stripe, can be used in the block.

A fabric motif, as a medallion, is perfect for the cornerstone. The size of the motif should be 2" of a 2 1/2" square. You need additional cornerstone fabric.

The side and corner triangle fabric may be the same as the background in the block, or may be an additional light or medium fabric.

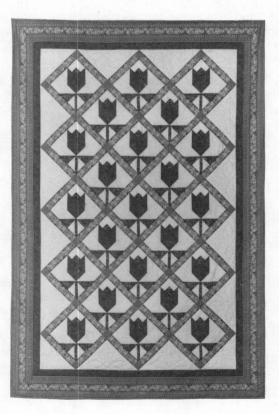

Cutting Measurement for Paste-Up Blocks Only

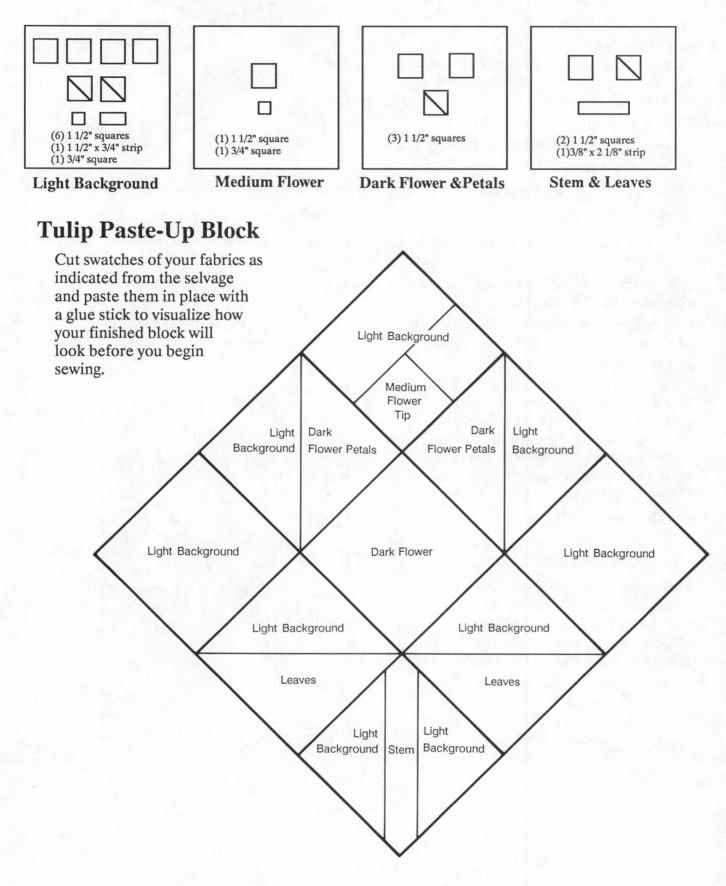

(6) 1 1/2" squares
(1) 1 1/2" x 3/4" strip
(1) 3/4" square

Light Background

(1) 1 1/2" square
(1) 3/4" square

Medium Flower

(3) 1 1/2" squares

Dark Flower &Petals

(2) 1 1/2" squares
(1)3/8" x 2 1/8" strip

Stem & Leaves

Tulip Paste-Up Block

Cut swatches of your fabrics as indicated from the selvage and paste them in place with a glue stick to visualize how your finished block will look before you begin sewing.

Light Background

Medium Flower Tip

Light Background — Dark Flower Petals — Dark Flower Petals — Light Background

Light Background — Dark Flower — Light Background

Light Background — Light Background

Leaves — Leaves

Light Background — Stem — Light Background

Cutting Tools and Techniques

Use a large industrial size rotary cutter and fresh blade with a 6" x 24" ruler to cut strips on an 18" x 24" gridded cutting mat. Use a 12 1/2" Square Up ruler when cutting squares larger than 6". Use a 6" square ruler for cutting squares smaller than 6".

Starting on page 10 refer to the Cutting Chart for your particular quilt size and setting.

Preparing to Cut the Fabric

Begin with the Light Background Fabric. Always trim away selvage edges before measuring.

1. Make a nick on the edge and tear from selvage to selvage to put the fabric on the straight-of-the-grain.

2. Fold the fabric in half, matching the torn straight edge thread to thread. It is often impossible to match the selvages.

3. Lay the fabric on the mat with most of it lying to the right. Line up the quarter inch line of the 6" x 24" ruler with the torn edge of the fabric on the left. Reverse this procedure if you are left-handed.

4. Spread the fingers of your left hand to hold the ruler firmly. With the rotary cutter in your right hand, begin cutting with the blade off the fabric on the mat. Put all your strength into the rotary cutter as you cut away from you, and trim the torn, ragged edge.

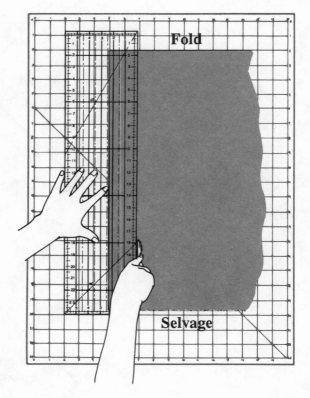

Cutting Narrow Strips

Begin by cutting 2 3/8" strips from the Light Background Fabric.

1. Move your ruler over until the 2 3/8" ruler lines are at the freshly cut edge. Cut the strip carefully and accurately. Repeat, cutting as many strips as indicated for your particular size quilt.

2. All narrow strips of the different fabrics and widths are cut in this manner. See page 49 for cutting striped fabric for the Lattice and Cornerstone Setting.

Cutting the Wider 9" Pieces and/or Strips

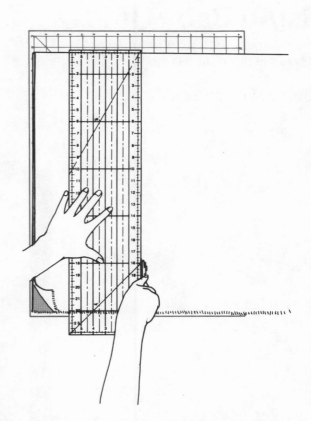

1. If your quilt needs only one 9" square of background, dark flower or leaf fabric, use the 12 1/2" Square Up ruler to measure and cut the piece.

2. If your quilt needs 9" wide strips less than 45", use the 6" x 24" ruler and the grid lines of the cutting mat to measure the size.

3. To cut 9" wide strips from 45" fabric, lay the folded and trimmed fabric along the 0" grid line on the cutting mat. Lay the 6" x 24" ruler along the 9" grid line. Cut the required number of background, dark flower and leaf 9" wide strips in this manner.

Cutting the 4" Squares

1. For the Baby Quilt and Lap Robe, the 4" squares are cut from the remaining light background fabric. It can be cut into 4" strips, and then into 4" squares.

2. On the larger quilts, cut 4" x 45" strips first from selvage to selvage with the 6" x 24" ruler, and then layer cut the 4" squares from the strips with the 6" square ruler. **Begin by trimming off and squaring the selvage edge**, and then cut toward the fold. You should get at least (10) 4" squares per strip.

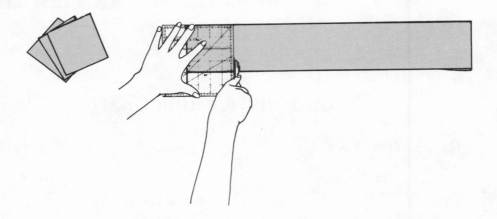

Cutting the 2 1/2" Square Cornerstones

The cornerstones are cut from 2 1/2" x 45" strips into 2 1/2" squares in the same manner as the 4" squares.

Tulip Baby Quilt
Four Blocks with a Solid Square
Approximate Finished Size 38" x 38"

Quilt by Loretta Smith

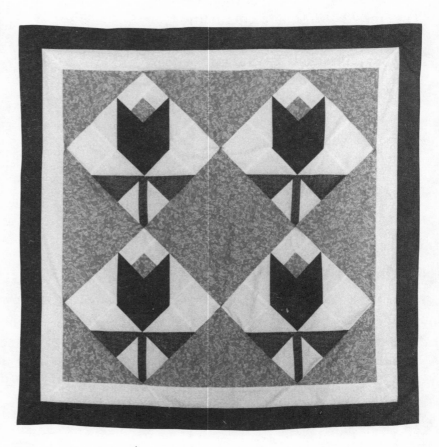

Yardage and Cutting Chart

Light Background		First Border	
1/2 yard	(1) 2 3/8" x 45" strip	1/3 yard	(4) 2" x 45" strips
	(2) 9" squares		
	(12) 4" squares		
Medium Flower Tip		**Second Border**	
1/8 yard	(1) 2 3/8" x 11" strip	5/8 yard	(4) 3 1/2" x 45" strips
Dark Flower/Petals		**Binding (optional)**	
1/3 yard	(1) 9" square	1/2 yard	(5) 3" x 45" strips
	(4) 4" squares		
Stem and Leaves		**Backing**	
1/3 yard	(1) 9" square	1 1/4 yards	One piece
	(1) 1 1/2" x 24" strip		
Solid Square*		**Bonded Batting**	
5/8 yard	Cut after Tulips are completed	45" x 45"	

*Includes Side and Corner Triangles

Tulip Baby Quilt

Five Blocks with
Lattice and Cornerstones
Approximate Finished Size 46" x 46"

Quilt by Eleanor Burns
with Border Variation

Yardage and Cutting Chart

Light Background		**First Border**	
1/2 yard	(1) 2 3/8" x 45" strip	1/3 yard	(4) 2" x 45" strips
	(2) 9" x 13 1/2" rectangles		
	(15) 4" squares		
Medium Flower Tip		**Second Border**	
1/8 yard	(1) 2 3/8" x 14" strip	2/3 yards	(5) 4" x 45" strips
Dark Flower/Petals		**Binding (optional)**	
1/3 yard	(1) 9" x 13 1/2" rectangle	1/2 yard	(5) 3" x 45" strips
	(5) 4" squares		
Stem and Leaves		**Backing**	
1/3 yard	(1) 9" x 13 1/2" rectangle	3 yards	Cut two 1 1/2 yard pieces
	(1) 1 1/2" x 30" strip		
Lattice (non-stripe)		**Bonded Batting**	
1/2 yard	(6) 2 1/2" x 45" strips	50" x 50"	
Cornerstones			
1/8 yard	(1) 2 1/2" x 45" strip into (12) 2 1/2" squares		
Side and Corner Triangles			
2/3 yard	Cut after Tulips are completed		

11

Tulip Lap Robe

Six Blocks with Solid Squares
Approximate Finished Size 39" x 54"

Quilt by Rosie Garcia

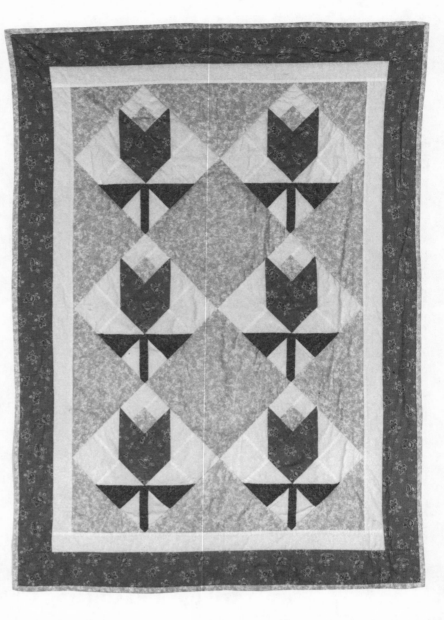

Yardage and Cutting Chart

Light Background		First Border	
3/4 yard	(1) 2 3/8" x 45" strip	3/8 yard	(4) 2 1/2" x 45" strips
	(2) 9" x 13 1/2" rectangles		
	(18) 4" squares		
Medium Flower Tip		**Second Border**	
1/8 yard	(1) 2 3/8" x 16" strip	3/4 yard	(5) 4" x 45" strips
Dark Flower/ Petals		**Binding (optional)**	
1/3 yard	(1) 9" x 13 1/2" rectangle	5/8 yard	(6) 3" x 45" strips
	(6) 4" squares		
Stem and Leaves		**Backing**	
1/3 yard	(1) 9" x 13 1/2" rectangle	1 5/8 yards in one piece	
	(2) 1 1/2" x 30" strips		
Solid Squares*		**Bonded Batting**	
7/8 yard	Cut after Tulips are completed	45" x 60"	

*Includes Side and Corner Triangles

Tulip Lap Robe
Eight Blocks with
Lattice and Cornerstones
Approximate Finished Size 48" x 65"

Quilt by Dee Dee Goodrich

Yardage and Cutting Chart

Light Background		**First Border**		
7/8 yard	(2) 2 3/8" x 45" strips	1/2 yard	(5) 2 1/2" x 45" strips	
	(2) 9" x 18" rectangles			
	(24) 4" squares			
Medium Flower Tip		**Second Border**		
1/8 yard	(1) 2 3/8" x 21" strip	7/8 yard	(6) 4" x 45" strips	
Dark Flower/Petals		**Binding (optional)**		
1/3 yard	(1) 9" x 18" rectangle	5/8 yard	(6) 3" x 45" strips	
	(8) 4" squares			
Stem and Leaves		**Backing**		
1/3 yard	(1) 9" x 18" rectangle	3 yards	Cut two 1 1/2 yard pieces	
	(2) 1 1/2" x 24" strips			
Lattice (non-stripe)		**Bonded Batting**		
2/3 yard	(8) 2 1/2" x 45" strips	54" x 72"		
Cornerstones				
1/8 yard	(1) 2 1/2" x 45" strip into (17) 2 1/2" squares			
Side and Corner Triangles				
1 yard	Cut after Tulips are completed			

Tulip Twin Quilt

Fifteen Blocks with Solid Squares
Approximate Finished Size 73" x 101"

Quilt by Anita Roberts

Yardage and Cutting Chart

Light Background 1 3/8 yards	(3) 2 3/8" x 45" strips (2) 9" x 45" strips (5) 4" x 45" strips into (45) 4" squares	**First Border** 3/4 yard	(6) 3 1/2" x 45" strips
Medium Flower Tip 1/8 yard	(1) 2 3/8" x 45" strip	**Second Border** 1 1/4 yards	(7) 5 1/2" x 45" strips
Dark Flower/Petals 5/8 yard	(1) 9" x 45" strip (2) 4" x 45" strips into (15) 4" squares	**Third Border** 2 yards	(9) 7 1/2" x 45" strips
Stem and Leaves 1/2 yard	(1) 9" x 45" strip (3) 1 1/2" x 45" strips	**Binding (optional)** 7/8 yard	(9) 3" x 45" strips
Solid Squares* 1 5/8 yards	Cut after Tulips are completed	**Backing** 6 yards	Two 3 yard pieces
		Bonded Batting 80" x 108"	

*Includes Side and Corner Triangles

Tulip Twin Quilt

Eleven Blocks with
Lattice and Cornerstones
Approximate Finished Size 66" x 100"

Quilt by Linda Phillips

Yardage and Cutting Chart

Light Background		**First Border**	
1 1/3 yards	(3) 2 3/8" x 45" strips	3/4 yard	(6) 3 1/2" x 45" strips
	(2) 9" x 45" strips		
	(4) 4" x 45" strips into (33) 4" squares		
Medium Flower Tip		**Second Border**	
1/8 yard	(1) 2 3/8" x 30" strip	1 1/4 yards	(7) 5 1/2" x 45" strips
Dark Flower/Petals		**Third Border**	
5/8 yard	(1) 9" x 45" strip	2 yards	(9) 7 1/2" x 45" strips
	(2) 4" x 45" strips into (11) 4" squares		
Stem and Leaves		**Binding (optional)**	
1/2 yard	(1) 9" x 45" strip	7/8 yard	(9) 3" x 45" strips
	(2) 1 1/2" x 45" strips		
Lattice (non-stripe)		**Backing**	
1 yard	(11) 2 1/2" x 45" strips	6 yards	Cut two 3 yard pieces
Cornerstones			
1/4 yard	(2) 2 1/2" x 45" strips into (22) 2 1/2" squares		
Side and Corner Triangles		**Bonded Batting**	
1 yard	Cut after Tulips are completed	72" x 108"	

Tulip Double Quilt

Twenty Blocks with Solid Squares
Approximate Finished Size 87" x 101"

Quilt by
Loretta Smith

Yardage and Cutting Chart

Light Background		**First Border**	
1 3/4 yards	(4) 2 3/8" x 45" strips	3/4 yard	(7) 3 1/2" x 45" strips
	(3) 9" x 45" strips		
	(6) 4" x 45" strips into (60) 4" squares		
Medium Flower Tip		**Second Border**	
1/4 yard	(1) 2 3/8" x 45" strip	1 1/3 yard	(8) 5 1/2" x 45" strips
	(1) 2 3/8" x 10" strip		
Dark Flower/Petals		**Third Border**	
7/8 yard	(2) 9" x 45" strips	2 yards	(9) 7 1/2" x 45" strips
	(2) 4" x 45" strips into (20) 4" squares		
Stem and Leaves		**Binding (optional)**	
2/3 yard	(2) 9" x 45" strips	7/8 yard	(9) 3" x 45" strips
	(3) 1 1/2" x 45" strips		
Solid Squares*		**Backing**	
2 1/4 yards	Cut after Tulips are completed	6 yards	Cut two 3 yard pieces
		Bonded Batting	
		90" x 108"	

*Includes Side and Corner Triangles

Tulip Double Quilt

Eighteen Blocks with
Lattice and Cornerstones
Approximate Finished Size 83" x 100"

Quilt by
Patricia Knoechel

Yardage and Cutting Chart

Light Background 1 5/8 yards	(4) 2 3/8" x 45" strips (2) 9" x 45" strips (6) 4" x 45" strips into (54) 4" squares	**First Border** 3/4 yard	(7) 3 1/2" x 45" strips
Medium Flower Tip 1/4 yard	(1) 2 3/8" x 45" strip (1) 2 3/8" x 5" strip	**Second Border** 1 1/3 yards	(8) 5 1/2" x 45" strips
Dark Flower/Petals 5/8 yard	(1) 9" x 45" strip (2) 4" x 45" strips into (18) 4" squares	**Third Border** 2 yards	(9) 7 1/2" x 45" strips
Stem and Leaves 1/2 yard	(1) 9" x 45" strip (3) 1 1/2" x 45" strips	**Binding (optional)** 7/8 yard	(9) 3" x 45" strips
Lattice (non-stripe) 1 1/4 yards	(16) 2 1/2" x 45" strips	**Backing** 6 yards	Cut two 3 yard pieces
Cornertones 1/4 yard	(2) 2 1/2" x 45" strips into (31) 2 1/2" squares		
Side and Corner Triangles 1 1/4 yards	Cut after Tulips are completed	**Bonded Batting** 90" x 108"	

Tulip Queen Quilt

For Twenty-Four Blocks with Solid Squares
Approximate Finished Size 87" x 115"

(The Queen quilt is extra long. If you plan to use shams with your quilt, refer to the Double quilt.)

Quilt by
Clara Muzio
with Border Variation

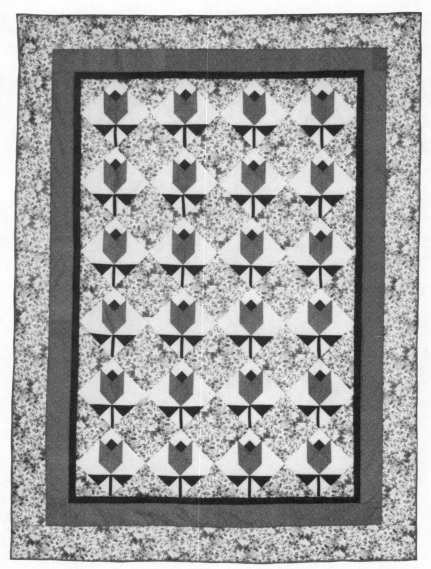

Yardage and Cutting Chart

Light Background		**First Border**	
2 yards	(4) 2 3/8" x 45" strips	7/8 yard	(8) 3 1/2" x 45" strips
	(3) 9" x 45" strips		
	(8) 4" x 45" strips into (72) 4" squares		
Medium Flower Tip		**Second Border**	
1/4 yard	(2) 2 3/8" x 45" strips	1 1/2 yards	(9) 5 1/2" x 45" strips
Dark Flower/Petals		**Third Border**	
1 yard	(2) 9" x 45" strips	2 1/3 yards	(10) 7 1/2" x 45" strips
	(3) 4" x 45" strips into (24) 4" squares		
Stem and Leaves		**Binding (optional)**	
3/4 yard	(2) 9" x 45" strips	1 yard	(10) 3" x 45" strips
	(4) 1 1/2" x 45" strips		
Solid Squares*		**Backing**	
2 1/2 yards	Cut after Tulips are completed	7 yards	Cut two 3 1/2 yard pieces
		Bonded Batting	
		90" x 120"	

*Includes Side and Corner Triangles

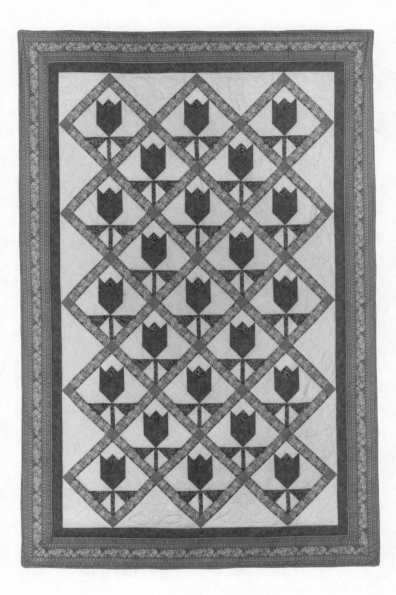

Tulip Queen Quilt
Twenty-Three Blocks with Lattice and Cornerstones
Approximate Finished Size 82" x 116"

(The Queen quilt is extra long. If you plan to use shams with your quilt, refer to the Double quilt.)

Quilt by
Eleanor Burns
with Border Variations

Yardage and Cutting Chart

Light Background		**First Border**	
2 yards	(5) 2 3/8" x 45" strips	7/8 yard	(8) 3 1/2" x 45" strips
	(3) 9" x 45" strips		
	(8) 4" x 45" strips into (69) 4" squares		
Medium Flower Tip		**Second Border**	
1/4 yard	(2) 2 3/8" x 45" strips	1 1/2 yards	(9) 5 1/2" x 45" strips
Dark Flower/Petals		**Third Border**	
1 yard	(2) 9" x 45" strips	2 1/3 yards	(10) 7 1/2" x 45" strips
	(3) 4" x 45" strips into (23) 4" squares		
Stem and Leaves		**Binding (optional)**	
3/4 yard	(2) 9" x 45" strips	1 yard	(10) 3" x 45" strips
	(4) 1 1/2" x 45" strips		
Lattice (non-stripe)		**Backing**	
1 5/8 yards	(20) 2 1/2" x 45" strips	7 yards	Cut two 3 1/2 yard pieces
Cornerstones			
1/3 yard	(3) 2 1/2" x 45" strips into (38) 2 1/2" squares		
Side and Corner Triangles		**Bonded Batting**	
1 1/4 yards	Cut after Tulips are completed	90" x 120"	

Tulip King Quilt

Thirty Blocks with Solid Squares
Approximate Finished Size 101" x 115"

Quilt by
Deborah Ward

Yardage and Cutting Chart

Light Background		**First Border**	
2 5/8 yards	(6) 2 3/8" x 45" strips	1 yard	(9) 3 1/2" x 45" strips
	(4) 9" x 45" strips		
	(9) 4" x 45" strips into (90) 4" squares		
Medium Flower Tip		**Second Border**	
1/4 yard	(2) 2 3/8" x 45" strips	1 1/2 yards	(9) 5 1/2" x 45" strips
Dark Flower/Petals		**Third Border**	
1 yard	(2) 9" x 45" strips	2 3/8 yards	(11) 7 1/2" x 45" strips
	(3) 4" x 45" strips into (30) 4" squares		
Stem and Leaves		**Binding (optional)**	
7/8 yard	(2) 9" x 45" strips	1 1/8 yards	(11) 3" x 45" strips
	(5) 1 1/2" x 45" strips		
Solid Squares*		**Backing**	
3 1/3 yards	Cut after Tulips are completed	9 yards	Cut three 3 yard pieces
		Bonded Batting	
		108" x 120"	

*Includes Side and Corner Triangles

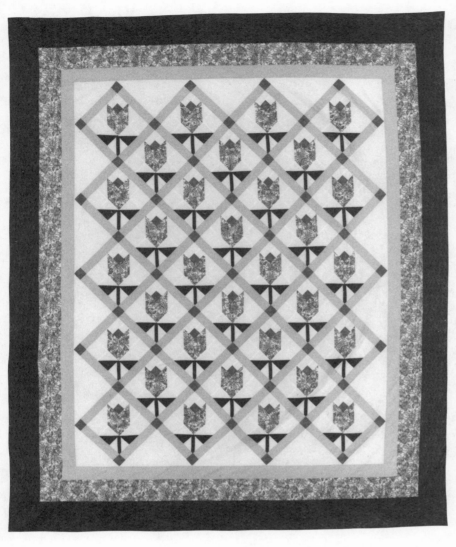

Tulip King Quilt

**Thirty-Two Blocks with
Lattice and Cornerstones**
Approximate Finished Size 99" x 116"

Quilt by
Kirsten Recce

Yardage and Cutting Chart

Light Background		**First Border**	
2 5/8 yards	(6) 2 3/8" x 45" strips	1 yard	(9) 3 1/2" x 45" strips
	(4) 9" x 45" strips		
	(9) 4" x 45" strips into (96) 4" squares		
Medium Flower Tip		**Second Border**	
1/4 yard	(2) 2 3/8" x 45" strips	1 3/4 yards	(10) 5 1/2" x 45" strips
Dark Flower/Petals		**Third Border**	
1 yard	(2) 9" x 45" strips	2 3/8 yards	(11) 7 1/2" x 45" strips
	(3) 4" x 45" strips into (32) 4" squares		
Stem and Leaves		**Binding (optional)**	
7/8 yard	(2) 9" x 45" strips	1 1/8 yards	(11) 3" x 45" strips
	(5) 1 1/2" x 45" strips		
Lattice (non-stripe)		**Backing**	
2 yards	(27) 2 1/2" x 45" strips	9 yards	Cut three 3 yard pieces
Cornerstones			
1/3 yard	(4) 2 1/2" x 45" strips into (49) 2 1/2" squares		
Side and Corner Triangles		**Bonded Batting**	
1 1/2 yards	Cut after Tulips are completed	108" x 120"	

Pillows, Pillow Shams and Dust Ruffle

Yardage and Cutting Chart

Pillow
Scrap Tulip Block (See page 5 for fabric measurements)

Corner Triangles		**Backing**	
1/3 yard	Cut (2) 8 1/4" squares Cut in half on the diagonal	5/8 yard	Cut when block is completed
Borders		**Bonded Batting**	
1/4 yard	Cut (2) 2 1/2" x 45" strips	(1) 20" square	
Lace Ruffle		**Two 1# Bags Polyester Stuffing**	
2 1/4 yards of 2 1/2" wide pregathered lace			

Two Pillow Shams   (Standard Size)

Pillow Casing	
2 1/2 yards	Cut (2) 20 1/2" x 28 1/2" for fronts *(Cut 28 1/2" lengthwise and then cut on fold)* Cut (4) 14" x 28 1/2" for backs
Ruffle	
1 3/4 yards	Cut (10) 6" x 45" strips
"No Show" Strong Cord or Crochet Thread	
14 yards	

Dust Ruffle

"No Show" Lining

Twin		Queen	
2 1/4 yards	Remains (1) piece	3 1/2 yards	Cut (2) equal pieces
Double		**King**	
3 1/4 yards	Cut (2) equal pieces	4 1/2 yards	Cut (2) equal pieces

Measure the drop from the top edge of the box spring to the floor before purchasing the yardage. Add 1/4" for the seam allowance plus 1/2" for the rolled hem.

Your Drop plus 3/4" ["]

The average height of a bed from the top of the box spring to the floor is 15". However, some beds sit closer to the floor because of a low frame, and may only be 13 1/2" from the floor. In this case, you will need less fabric.

In addition, check the width of the fabric you are purchasing for the ruffle. If it is less than 42" wide, you will need to follow the fabric requirements for 14" height or more regardless of the drop.

These yardage charts are based on 2 1/2 times ratio for fullness. You will need more fabric if you want a 3 times ratio.

Fabric for Dust Ruffle

Fabric is cut the measurement of your drop plus 3/4"

13 1/2" Ht. or Less		14" Ht. or More	
Twin			
4 1/4 yards	Cut (3) equal pieces	7 yards	Cut (2) equal pieces
Double			
5 yards	Cut (3) equal pieces	7 1/2 yards	Cut (2) equal pieces
Queen			
5 1/4 yards	Cut (3) equal pieces	7 3/4 yards	Cut (2) equal pieces
King			
4 1/2 yards	Cut (3) equal pieces	8 1/2 yards	Cut (2) equal pieces

General Sewing Instructions

Seam Allowance

Sew an accurate and consistent 1/4" seam allowance throughout the sewing of the quilt.

Conventional Sewing Machine Versus Serger

The tulip quilt can be made entirely on a conventional sewing machine. However, to speed the quilt making process, a serger can be used for specific parts of the sewing if the seam allowances on the two machines can be matched thread to thread.

 ### Seam Allowance for Conventional Sewing Machine

The width of the presser foot usually determines the seam allowance. Line the edges of the fabric with the edge of the presser foot and sew a few stitches. Measure the seam allowance. If it is 1/4", a **magnetic seam guide** placed on the metal throat plate against the presser foot will assure a consistent 1/4" seam. If the measurement is less than 1/4", place the magnetic seam guide at a slight distance from the presser foot for a consistent 1/4". If the seam allowance measures more than 1/4", you may be able to adjust the needle position or feed the fabric so that it doesn't come to the edge of the presser foot.

 ### Seam Allowance for Serger

If available, use the fabric guide attachment on the serger, and make the seam adjustment by moving the guide. Do not let the serger's knife trim the edges.

Conventional seam

Matched seams

Serger seam

The serger is faster to use when sewing the flower tip together. Because of diagonal sewing across the fabric, the conventional sewing machine must be used when sewing the petals and leaves. The serger can be used again when setting the quilt together and adding borders.

Stitches Per Inch

Set your machine at a tight stitch, **15 stitches per inch,** or #2 to #2.5 on machines with stitch selections from #1 - #4. This small stitch is used because backstitching is rarely done.

Making Patches with Medium Flower Tips

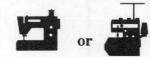 **You need:**

- 2 3/8" light background strips
- 2 3/8" medium flower strips

Make one flower tip patch for each tulip block in your quilt.

1. Place the 2 3/8" medium flower strip right sides together to the 2 3/8" light background strip.
2. Sew together lengthwise.

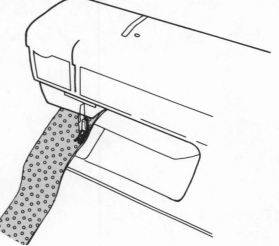

Depending on the size and setting of your quilt, sew the indicated length of medium and light strips together.

	Solid Square Setting	Lattice and Cornerstone Setting
Baby	Four Blocks	Five Blocks
	11"	14"
Lap	Six Blocks	Eight Blocks
	16"	21"
Twin	Fifteen Blocks	Eleven Blocks
	44"	30"
Double	Twenty Blocks	Eighteen Blocks
	44" plus 10"	44" plus 5"
Queen	Twenty-four Blocks	Twenty-three Blocks
	44" plus 20"	44" plus 16"
King	Thirty Blocks	Thirty-two Blocks
	44" twice	44" twice

3. Press the seam toward the medium strip.

4. Square off the left end. Cut into 2 3/8" sections. Stack.

5. Place the stack, right side down, to the left of your sewing machine.

6. Place a light background strip, right side up, in your sewing machine.

7. Place a 2 3/8" section right sides together to the light background strip with light end first. Stitch.

8. Butt the next sections behind the first until you have one patch for each tulip block in your quilt. If there is not enough strip to fit the section, start with another strip.

9. Cut apart between the patches.

10. From the wrong side, press the seam away from the light strip.

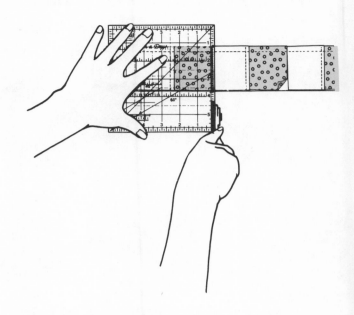

Squaring Up the Patch to 4"

1. Line up the 4" grid on the ruler to the outside corner of the medium square.

2. Line up the diagonal line down the center of the patch.

3. Trim on two sides, squaring up each patch to 4".

∗Scrap Patches Only∗

Making Scrap Patches with Medium Flower Tips

Making the medium flower tip patches from an assortment of fabrics is identical to the technique just described with this exception: Instead of using 2 3/8" strips of the medium flower, 2 3/8" squares are sewn to the 2 3/8" light background strips.

Making Dark Flower Petal Patches

 You need:

- 9" light background strips
- 9" dark flower petal strips

Make two flower patches for each tulip block in your quilt.

One 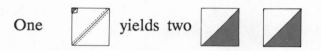 yields two

Baby and Lap Quilts: The 9" pieces have already been cut to size as instructed on the Cutting Charts. Begin at #3.

1. Place a 9" x 45" strip of light background fabric **right sides together** to a 9" x 45" strip of the dark flower petal fabric. Press with the light on top.

2. Position the gridded cutting mat so that zero is in the left hand bottom corner. Place the edge of the 9" layered strips on the gridded cutting mat in that corner slightly to the left of zero. **Trim off the selvage edges at zero.**

The number of 9" strips and grid sizes depend on the size and setting of your quilt.

Number and Size of Grid Per Quilt

	Solid Block Setting	Lattice and Cornerstone Setting
Baby	Four Blocks	Five Blocks
	(1) 9" x 9"	(1) 9" x 13 1/2"
Lap	Six Blocks	Eight Blocks
	(1) 9" x 13 1/2"	(1) 9" x 18"
Twin	Fifteen Blocks	Eleven Blocks
	(2) 9" x 18"	(2) 9" x 13 1/2"
Double	Twenty Blocks	Eighteen Blocks
	(2) 9" x 18"	(1) 9" x 18"
	(1) 9" x 9"	(1) 9" x 22 1/2"
Queen	Twenty-four Blocks	Twenty-three Blocks
	(3) 9" x 18"	(3) 9" x 18"
King	Thirty Blocks	Thirty-two Blocks
	(4) 9" x 18"	(4) 9" x 18"

3. Draw **vertical lines every 4 1/2"** along the grid. According to your particular size quilt and setting, cut pieces at required sizes. Remove any excess.

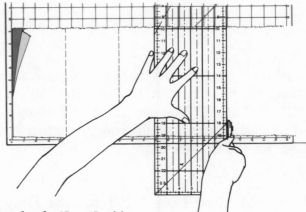

Example of a 9" x 18" grid.

Draw a line every 4 1/2", and then cut at 18".

4. Draw a horizontal line **at 4 1/2".**

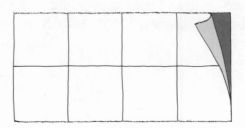

5. Draw **diagonal lines** starting in the bottom right corner **every other diagonal row**.

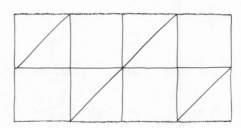

6. Draw **diagonal lines in the opposite direction** in the remaining unmarked rows.

You will be using a combination of these grids found in the Cutting Charts depending on the number of patches needed for your quilt. These sizes are designed for sewing ease.

Examples of Various Grid Sizes

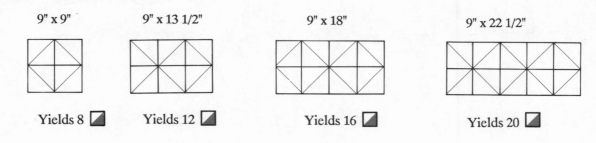

9" x 9"	9" x 13 1/2"	9" x 18"	9" x 22 1/2"
Yields 8	Yields 12	Yields 16	Yields 20

For instance, the king size quilt needs (4) 9" x 18" pieces of layered light and dark. After squaring off the left end of the layered 9" strips, draw vertical lines at 4 1/2", 9", and 13 1/2". Cut at 18". You can get an additional 9" x 18" piece from the same 9" strip. You need a second 9" strip for the remaining two 9" x 18" pieces. The excess can be cut into 4" squares for the tulip block.

Marking a Dashed Line 1/4" from the Diagonal Lines

To help you get started with your sewing, find the long 1/4" line marked along the edge of your ruler.

1. Place this 1/4" line on top of your drawn line in the bottom right "diamond." Draw a dashed sewing line 1/4" away from the solid line through this one square. This is your guide line for sewing.

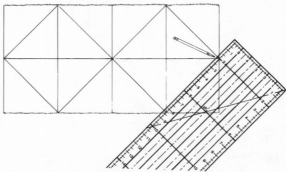

2. Pin the two pieces together in the center of each marked triangle.

Sewing 1/4" from the Diagonal Lines

 Use a neutral color of thread in the bobbin and on top of your machine.

1. Begin sewing on the dashed sewing line. Maintain this seam allowance throughout your sewing. Depending on the width of your presser foot, you may line up the edge of the foot with the diagonal line.

2. At the end of the first line, pivot the strip with the needle in the fabric at the grid line, and continue sewing 1/4" from the diagonal line.

3. Sew a 1/4" seam on the other side of the diagonal line. Do not backstitch.

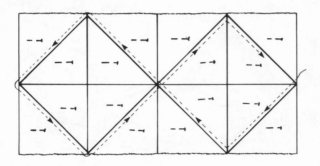 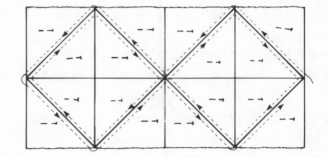

Continuously sew, pivoting the fabric until you reach the point where you began sewing.

4. Remove pins and press.

Cutting the Patches Apart

1. Lay the stitched piece on the cutting mat. With the rotary cutter and 6" x 24" ruler, cut apart on the 4 1/2" square lines. Cut apart on all the diagonal lines exactly as you marked them.

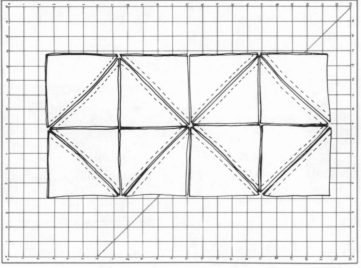

If you leave the piece lying flat on the mat, you can make long cuts, and cut them apart very quickly.

Pressing the Seams to the Dark Side

Use steam at a cotton setting on your iron.

1. Stack the pieces into several piles. Do not open the pieces. Place the piles on the ironing board with light sides on the bottom.

2. Drop one piece in the center of the ironing board with the light side on the bottom.

3. Lift up the dark part and press it open and flat. Do not put down the iron.

4. Lay a second piece on top of the first with light side down again. Press it open and flat.

5. Continue to press without putting down the iron; stack as you press the piece. The dark and light will always be in the same position.

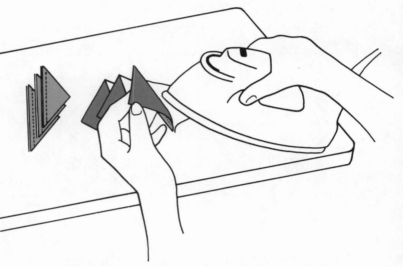

Squaring Each Patch to 4"

1. Place the upper right corner of the 6" x 6" ruler on top of your patch.

2. Line up the 45° line on the ruler with the diagonal seam on the patch.

3. Match the 4" grid with the edge of the block. Trim off any irregular edges on two sides.

4. Turn your patch in the opposite direction. Straighten the two remaining sides.

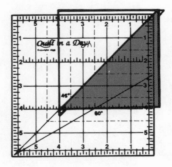
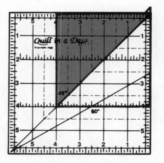

Be sure the seam runs exactly into the corners.

Making Green Leaf Patches

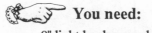 **You need:**

- 9" light background strips
- 9" green leaf strips

Make two green leaf patches for each block in your quilt.

The green leaf patches are made identical to the dark flower patches. Repeat these instructions.

∗Scrap Patches Only∗

Making Scrap Dark Flower Petal and Green Leaf Patches

The technique for making scrap dark flower and green leaf patches is similar to the grid technique described, with the exception of sewing 1/4" from the diagonal lines on 4 1/2" squares instead of sewing 1/4" from the diagonal lines marked on a multiple 4 1/2" grid.

1. Draw a diagonal line on the **wrong side** of each 4 1/2" dark flower petal square and green leaf square. You need one of each for each tulip block.

2. Cut the 9" x 45" light background strips into 4 1/2" x 45" strips.

3. Place one 4 1/2" dark flower petal square right sides together to a 4 1/2" light background strip. Pin.

4. Line up and pin all remaining squares onto the strip as shown. It may be necessary to use additional light strips.

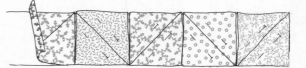

5. Continuously sew a 1/4" seam on one side of the diagonal line, pivoting with the needle in the fabric.

6. At the opposite end of the strip, turn the strip around and sew on the other side of the diagonal line.

7. Remove the pins, and press.

8. Cut, press open, and square as instructed.

Making Light Patches with Stems

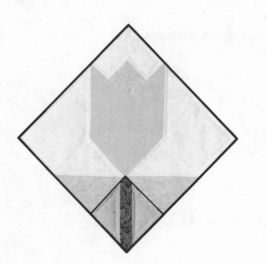

 You need:

- one 4" light background square for each tulip block in your quilt
- 1 1/2" wide stem strips
- iron
- pins
- optional 18 mm. bias tape maker
- optional invisible thread

Make one stem patch for each tulip block in your quilt.

The raw edges of the stem strip are pressed under and then sewn to the light square on the diagonal. Select the technique you prefer:

Pressing with an iron

Pressing with an iron and straight pin

Pressing with an iron and bias tape maker

Pressing with an Iron

1. Place the 1 1/2" wide stem strip on the ironing board with the wrong side up.
2. Fold the long raw edges to meet in the center. Press, forming a "bias tape looking" strip about 3/4" wide.
3. Press on the right side.

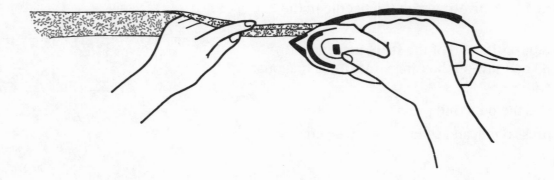

Pressing with an Iron and Straight Pin

1. Repeat the previous steps, pressing only 6" of the strip.
2. Place a long quilter's straight pin into the ironing board cover with approximately a 3/4" length of pin exposed in the center.
3. Pull the pressed end through the straight pin with wrong side up.
4. Place the iron flat on the board to the left of the pin.
5. Carefully pull the strip under the pin and the iron with your left hand as you fold the raw edges to the center with your right hand.

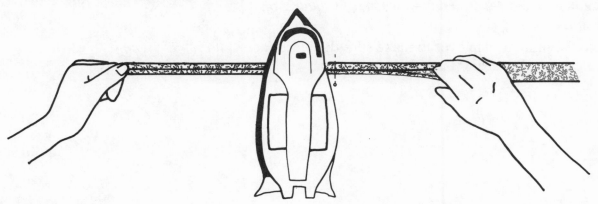

Pressing with an Iron and Bias Tape Maker

You need an 18 millimeter bias tape maker for this process.

1. Cut the end of the strip on the diagonal.
2. With the help of a straight pin, start the diagonal cut end wrong side up through the wide open end of the bias tape maker. **Arrange the strip so it is centered.**
3. Straight pin the cut end to the ironing board cover.

4. Placing the iron in your right hand, grasp the handle on the bias tape maker in your left hand.
5. Pull the bias tape maker away from the iron, turning the edges in and pressing the strip flat at the same time.

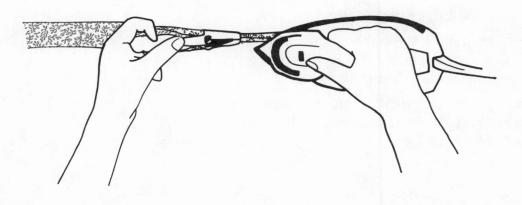

Pinning the Light Squares to the Stem Strips

1. Lay out the pressed stem strip with wrong side up.

2. Diagonally center a 4" light square on the strip with wrong side up. Make certain that the corners of the square line up with the center of the strip.

3. Carefully pin each end of the square.

   It is crucial that the stems are centered.

4. Pin all needed squares in a row wrong sides up on the diagonal. *If needed, you can fit seven light squares on a 45" strip.*

5. Turn the pinned strip over to make sure the pieces are pinned flat. Pin again if necessary.

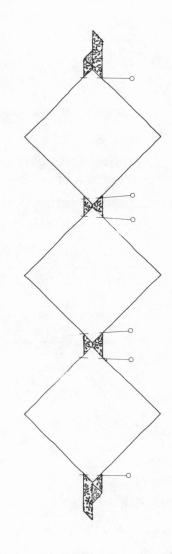

Anchoring Both Edges of the Stem Strips

The edges of the stem strips are anchored to the light background squares on the diagonal. For the most attractive finished look, use thread to match the stem fabric, and/or soft 100% nylon invisible thread. If you use invisible thread, use it on the top only, and loosen the top tension. Choose the technique you prefer:

Straight Edge Stitch Method

Zigzag Stitch Method

Blind Hem or Blanket Stitch Method

Straight Edge Stitch Method

Use bobbin and top thread to match your stem fabric, or use invisible thread in your top, and bobbin thread to match the stem.

Move your needle position and/or line up your presser foot so you can edge stitch 1/16" away from the folded edge.

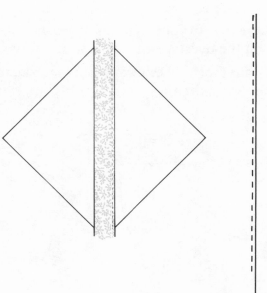

Zigzag Stitch Method

Use bobbin and top thread to match your stem fabric or invisible thread in your top, and bobbin thread to match the stem.

Set your machine with a narrow zigzag width and short stitch length. Line up your needle position and/or presser foot so that the zigzag stitches catch the folded edge.

Blind Hem or Blanket Stitch Method

Use bobbin thread to match the light square and invisible thread on top.

Select the blind hem stitch or blanket stitch that bites to the left. Set your machine with a narrow width and short stitch length. Move your needle position and/or line up your presser foot so the straight stitch is on the light square, and the bite is on the stem strip.

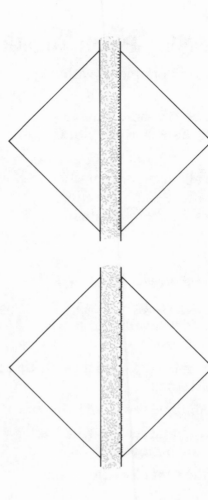

Sewing the Stem Strips

1. Sew down one side of all stems, turn, and sew back up the other side.

2. From the wrong side, trim the stems to match the corners on the 4" squares. You may find the 6" square ruler useful when trimming.

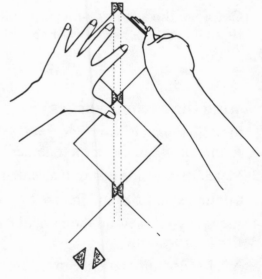

3. **From the wrong side carefully trim** away the folded green stem fabric and the corner of the light background square at both ends.

4. Set aside.

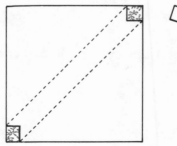

Sewing the Nine-Patch Together

1. Lay out the patchwork pieces with the 4" squares.

   There should be the same number of pieces in each stack as are blocks in the quilt.

2. Make certain all pieces are consistently turned in the same direction. The pieces are numbered in their sewing order.

Sewing the First Vertical Seams

1. Flip #2 right sides togther to #1. Flip #4 right sides together to #3. Flip #6 right sides together to #5.

2. Pick up pieces #1/#2. Match the outside edges, backstitch, and stitch.

3. Pick up and continue sewing #3/#4 after #1/#2.

4. Pick up and continue sewing #5/#6 after #3/#4. Backstitch at the bottom of #5/#6.

5. Repeat with the next block in the quilt. Do not clip the threads.

   Continue the assembly-line until all pieces in the first two vertical rows have been stitched into a long chain.

Sewing the Second Vertical Seams

1. Flip the top piece from stack #7 right sides together to the top #2 in the sewn together chain.

2. Match the outside edges, backstitch, and stitch.

3. Continue with #8, and then #9.

4. Assembly-line sew all the remaining pieces in the third vertical row.

5. After every third patch, clip the threads connecting the blocks.

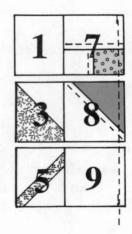

Check to see that all pieces are turned correctly. Stack the blocks.

Sewing the First Horizontal Seams

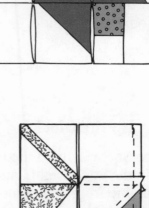

1. Position the stack of blocks as shown. Check the detail on how the sewn together patches look.

2. Flip the first row right sides together to the second row.

3. Match the seams, turning the top seams up and the underneath seams down.

4. Assembly line sew all the blocks in the stack.

   Do not clip the blocks apart.

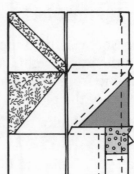

Sewing the Second Horizontal Seams

Turn the chain around and start with the last block in the chain.

1. Stitch the first seam by matching the seam, turning the top seam down, and turning the underneath seam up.

2. **A critical point to match is where the two leaves meet at the stem**. As you approach this seam, shown by an arrow, lift up the stem piece to see the right sides. Carefully line up the two leaves before stitching.

3. Stitch the remaining horizontal seams in this manner.

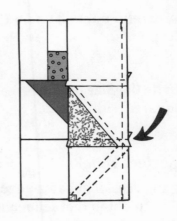

Pressing the Block

1. From the wrong side, press the seams away from the stem.

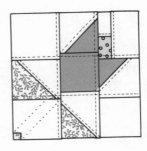

2. Press from the right side.

Squaring Up the Block

1. Place the Square Up on top of the block. Place the 1" line in the upper right hand corner. Line up the diagonal line from one corner to the next. Remember the size of the block.

2. Measure several tulip blocks to find an average measurement.

3. Square all your blocks to this measurement by first matching the 1/4" line on the ruler to the points. Carefully trim and straighten the two outside edges. Turn the block, match the 1/4" line to the points, and straighten the two remaining sides.

Be careful not to trim away the seam allowance on the points.

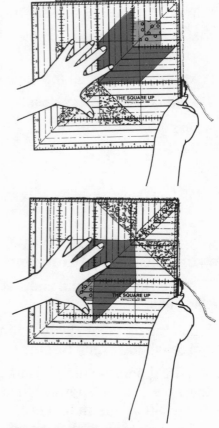

Write the Size of Your Squared Tulip Block

Imperfect Blocks

If an occasional patch edge is shy of the measurement, mark it with a pin, and make an adjustment in that seam allowance when sewing the top together.

If some of the blocks are not perfect squares, they will appear straight once they are sewn together into a top.

Continue on the next page for setting tulip blocks together with solid squares.

Turn to page 49 for setting tulip blocks together with lattice and cornerstones.

Setting the Quilt Together with Solid Squares

This setting does not have lattice and cornerstones.

To finish your quilt top, you need to cut the pieces for the Side Triangles, Corner Triangles, and Solid Squares from the Solid Square fabric listed on your Yardage Chart. **The largest pieces are cut first.**

The Side Triangles

The side triangles come from cutting large squares on both diagonals into four triangles. The size of these squares is based on the size of your tulip block from page 40.

If your Tulip Block is:	Then cut this size of square:
10 1/2" - 10 5/8"	15 1/2"
10 3/4" - 10 7/8"	16"
11"	16 1/4"

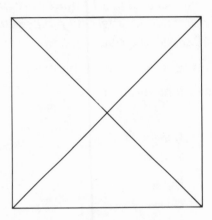

1. Trim selvages. Cut squares this size in the quantity needed.

Baby - 1 square	**Double - 4 squares**
Lap - 2 squares	**Queen - 4 squares**
Twin - 3 squares	**King - 5 squares**

Cut carefully without wasting fabric. Use the 6" x 24" ruler and gridded mat. Side strips of fabric can be used for the corner triangles and solid squares.

2. Cut into fourths on both diagonals with the rotary cutter and 6" x 24" ruler. These diagonal cuts are on the bias. **The triangles should be handled carefully so the bias does not stretch.**

When the side triangles are sewn into the quilt, the bias is on the inside, and the straight-of-the-grain is on the outside edge of the quilt.

The Corner Triangles

The four corner triangles come from cutting two squares on the diagonal. The size of the two squares is based on the size of your tulip block. Cut squares in half on the diagonal.

If your Tulip Block is:	Then cut this size of two squares:
10 1/2" - 10 5/8"	8"
10 3/4" - 10 7/8"	8 1/4"
11"	8 1/2"

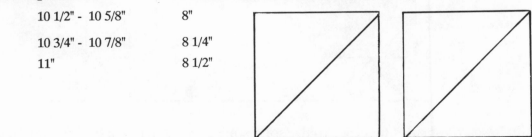

The Solid Squares

The solid squares are the same size as your tulip blocks. Use the 6" x 24" ruler for cutting the strips at that width, and the 12 1/2" Square Up ruler for cutting the strips into squares.

Baby - 1 square	**Double** - (3) 45" strips into 12 squares
Lap - 2 squares	**Queen** - (4) 45" strips into 15 squares
Twin - (2) 45" strips into 8 squares	**King** - (5) 45" strips into 20 squares

Assembly-Line Sewing the Blocks Together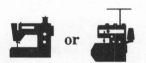

The tulip blocks and solid squares are first assembly-line sewn into pairs, then sewn into multiples of pairs with a single tulip block until each diagonal row has the necessary number of blocks. After the diagonal rows are sewn, the side and corner triangles are added.

1. Lay out equal piles of tulip blocks and solid squares **in this order**.

   Place this many in each stack:

   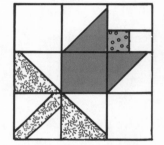

   Baby - 1
   Lap - 2
   Twin - 8
   Double - 12
   Queen - 15
   King - 20

   Set the extras aside.

2. Flip the solid square right sides together to the tulip block. Match and pin the outside edges.

3. Sew together, being careful to stitch across the points on the tulip block so they remain "crisp" from the right side. **Sew the seams of the patches as pressed.**

4. Assembly-line sew all pairs. Clip the threads holding them together.

5. Lay out equal piles of the sewn together pairs and single tulip blocks **in this order**.

   Place this many in each stack:

   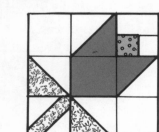 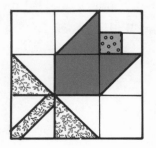

   Baby - 1
   Lap - 2
   Twin - 2
   Double - 2
   Queen - 2
   King - 2

6. Flip the tulip block right sides together to the solid square. Match, pin, and sew together.
   These three block rows are the middle rows for the baby and lap; and are the second rows in from the top left and bottom right corners of the larger quilts.

7. **Refer to the illustration of your size quilt on the following pages.** Position these completed rows on a large floor or table area.

   The baby quilt and lap robe are now ready for the single blocks, side, and corner triangles. Skip steps #8 and #9.

8. Lay out equal piles of sewn together pairs **in this order.**

   Place this many in each stack:

   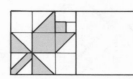 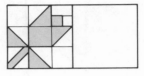

   Twin - 3

   Double - 4

   Queen - 5

   King - 8

9. Assembly-line sew them together.

   Following your quilt illustration, continue to sew pairs of blocks together, adding single tulips to the end of each row until you have the number of blocks needed in each row. Press seam toward the solid blocks. Lay completed rows into position.

10. Place a corner triangle in each corner. Place side triangles around the outside forming a straight edge.

BABY QUILT

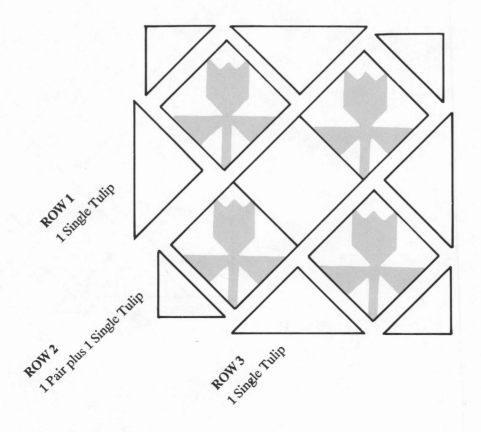

ROW 1
1 Single Tulip

ROW 2
1 Pair plus 1 Single Tulip

ROW 3
1 Single Tulip

LAP ROBE

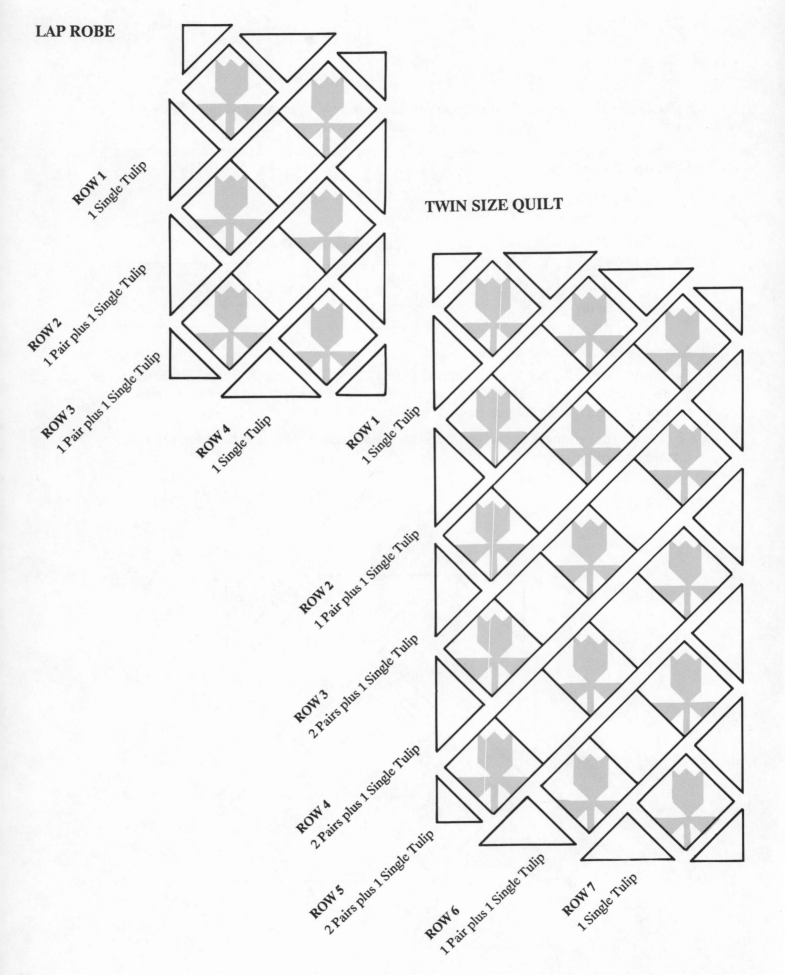

ROW 1
1 Single Tulip

ROW 2
1 Pair plus 1 Single Tulip

ROW 3
1 Pair plus 1 Single Tulip

ROW 4
1 Single Tulip

TWIN SIZE QUILT

ROW 1
1 Single Tulip

ROW 2
1 Pair plus 1 Single Tulip

ROW 3
2 Pairs plus 1 Single Tulip

ROW 4
2 Pairs plus 1 Single Tulip

ROW 5
2 Pairs plus 1 Single Tulip

ROW 6
1 Pair plus 1 Single Tulip

ROW 7
1 Single Tulip

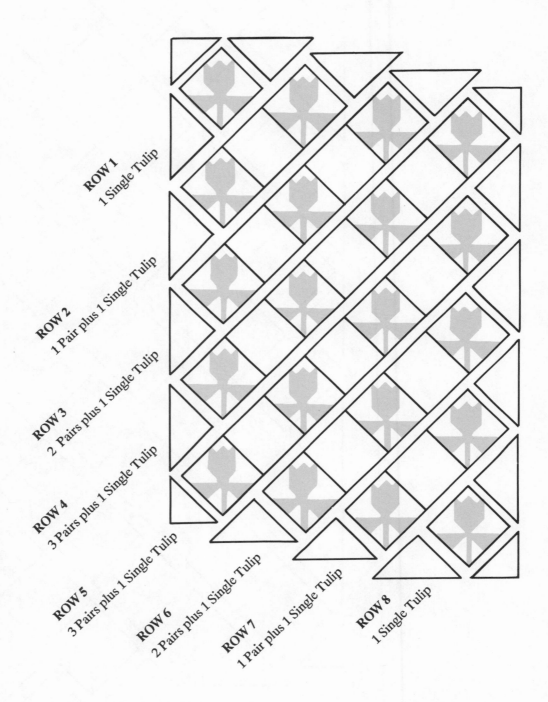

ROW 1
1 Single Tulip

ROW 2
1 Pair plus 1 Single Tulip

ROW 3
2 Pairs plus 1 Single Tulip

ROW 4
3 Pairs plus 1 Single Tulip

ROW 5
3 Pairs plus 1 Single Tulip

ROW 6
2 Pairs plus 1 Single Tulip

ROW 7
1 Pair plus 1 Single Tulip

ROW 8
1 Single Tulip

QUEEN SIZE QUILT

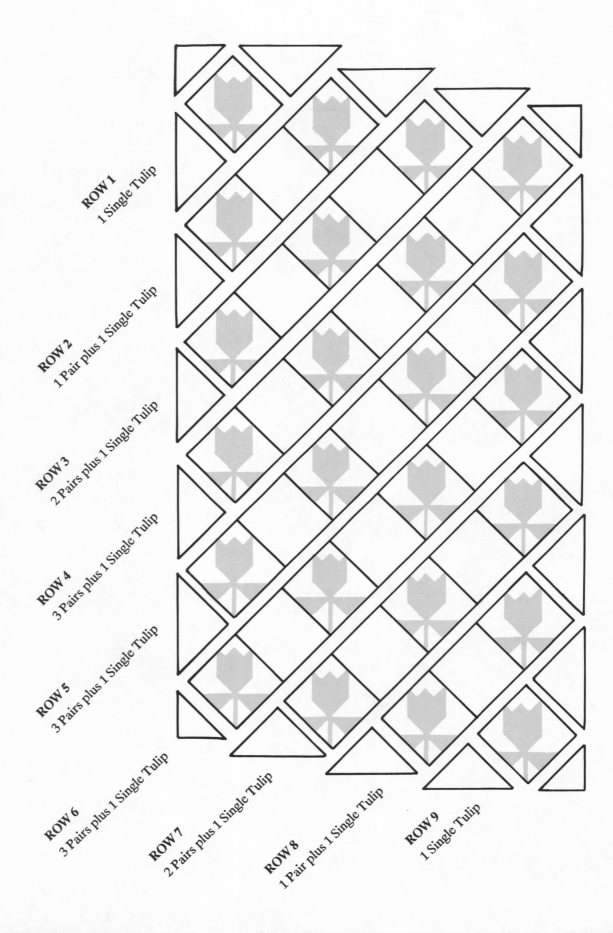

ROW 1
1 Single Tulip

ROW 2
1 Pair plus 1 Single Tulip

ROW 3
2 Pairs plus 1 Single Tulip

ROW 4
3 Pairs plus 1 Single Tulip

ROW 5
3 Pairs plus 1 Single Tulip

ROW 6
3 Pairs plus 1 Single Tulip

ROW 7
2 Pairs plus 1 Single Tulip

ROW 8
1 Pair plus 1 Single Tulip

ROW 9
1 Single Tulip

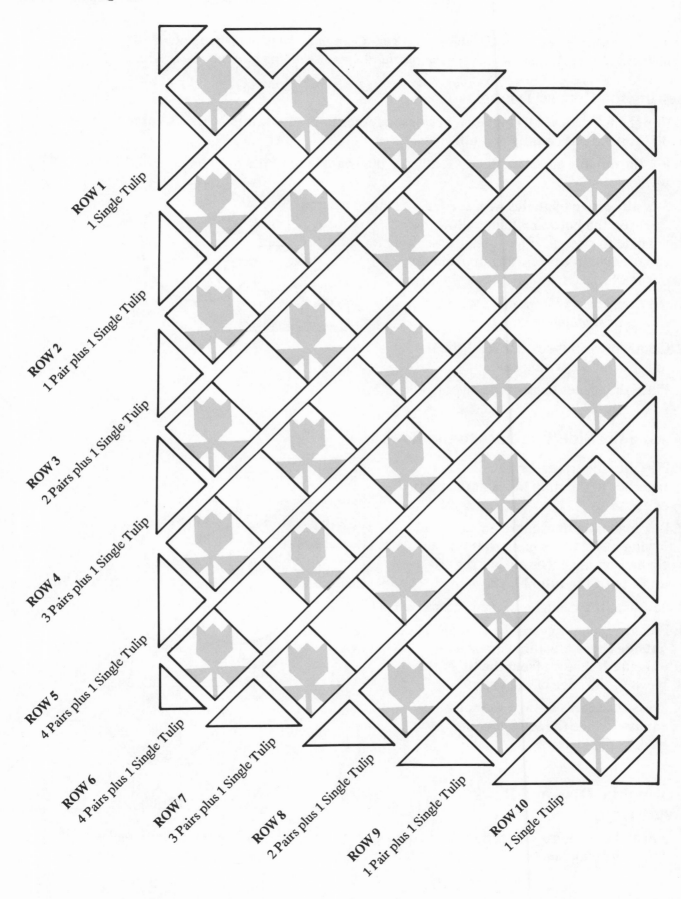

ROW 1
1 Single Tulip

ROW 2
1 Pair plus 1 Single Tulip

ROW 3
2 Pairs plus 1 Single Tulip

ROW 4
3 Pairs plus 1 Single Tulip

ROW 5
4 Pairs plus 1 Single Tulip

ROW 6
4 Pairs plus 1 Single Tulip

ROW 7
3 Pairs plus 1 Single Tulip

ROW 8
2 Pairs plus 1 Single Tulip

ROW 9
1 Pair plus 1 Single Tulip

ROW 10
1 Single Tulip

The corner and side triangles have bias edges. Care must be taken when sewing so that the triangles do not stretch and distort the outside edge. A walking foot may be useful.

Sewing the Corner Triangles

1. Flip the four corner triangles right sides together to the four tulip blocks. **Center so that 3/8" tips extend equally on both sides.**

2. **Pin the outside edges in place.** Gently pat the triangle to fit the tulip block. **Pin the center.**

3. **Sew all corner triangles with the triangle on the bottom.** Do not allow the triangle to stretch. If necessary, ease the triangle to fit by lifting up from underneath.

   Be careful not to "trim off" the points with your stitching lines.

4. Gently press this seam toward the triangle from the wrong side.

5. Place the pieces back in the layout.

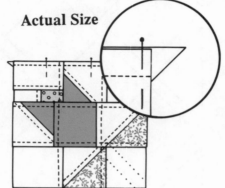

Actual Size

Sewing the Side Triangles to the Rows

1. Flip the side triangle right sides together to the tulip block at the ends of each row.

2. Pin, matching the square edge, and **allowing a 3/8" tip to hang over on the corner triangle. Gently pat the triangle to fit the tulip block.**

3. Sew with the triangle on the bottom.

4. Press the seam toward the triangle. **The outside edges must line up. Allow only the 1/4" seam from the tip of the block to the edge of the top.**

5. **Press the seams toward the solid square.** Place the sewn together row back in the layout.

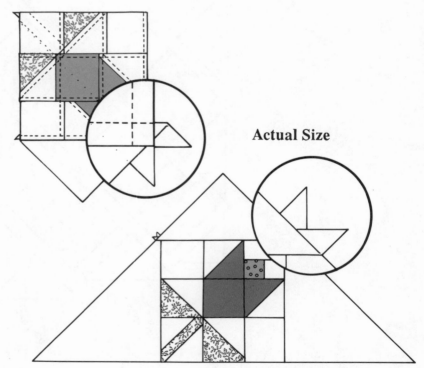

Actual Size

Sewing the Diagonal Rows Together

Pin and sew the rows together into a quilt top. *Sew with the bulk of the quilt to the left of the sewing machine, so seams can easily be checked.*

Setting the Quilt Together with Lattice and Cornerstones

Cutting Striped Fabric for the Lattice (Optional)

Striped fabric is cut with the grain lengthwise rather than selvage to selvage. The stripe you select should be 2" wide plus a 1/4" seam allowance on each side, and is cut the length of the block, which is approximately 10 1/2" to 11".

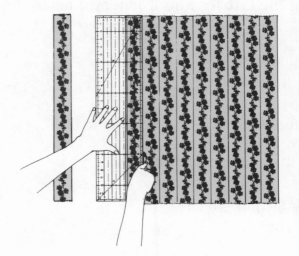

1. Unfold the fabric and place it on the gridded mat. Consistently cut the stripe into the planned design one layer at a time, using the 6" x 24" ruler.

2. A lattice is cut the measurement of your tulip block. Check the Chart below for how many lattice you need. Figure your yardage by the number of useable stripes.

   For instance: a stripe cut lengthwise from 2/3 yards fabric is 24" long. You can get (2) lattice from one stripe. Because the stripe is cut lengthwise with the grain and does not "give," you may want to cut each lattice 1/8" longer than your tulip block.

Cutting and Arranging the Lattice

1. Refer to page 40 for the measurement of your tulip block.

2. Layer the 2 1/2" x 45" strips cut from the lattice fabric. **Trim off the selvages.**

3. Cut each lattice the measurement of your block. You should get three lattice from each 45" strip. If you can get four lattice from a strip, you will need to cut fewer strips.

   Cut this many lattice for your quilt:

Baby - 16	**Double** - 48
Lap - 24	**Queen** - 60
Twin - 32	**King** - 80

4. **Make two stacks equal to the number of tulip blocks**. Set the remaining lattice aside.

5. **Make one stack of cornerstones** equal to the number of tulip blocks. Set the remaining cornerstones aside.

6. Place the counted pieces **in this order:**

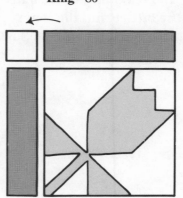

Sewing the Lattice and Cornerstones to the Tulip Blocks

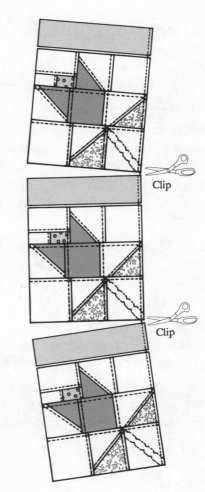

1. Flip the top lattice right sides together to the cornerstone. Sew.

2. Flip the block right sides together to the lattice. Match the outside edges, butt to the lattice/cornerstone, and sew.

3. **Assembly-line sew** all the pieces together in this order.

4. **Clip the threads after every tulip block.**

5. Open flat and stack right side up.

6. Flip the cornerstone and lattice right sides together to the tulip block. Match the seam, **pushing the seam allowance underneath toward the lattice and the seam allowance on top toward the lattice.** Sew.

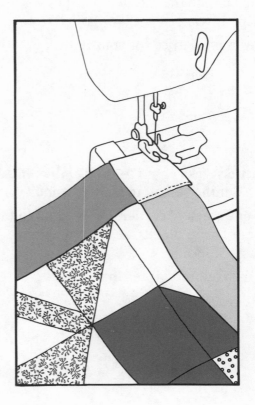

7. **Assembly-line sew all the pieces.**

8. Clip apart the threads holding the tulips together according to the number of tulip blocks in each diagonal row:

Number of Tulip Blocks in Diagonal Rows

Baby	**Double**
Clip after 1, 3, and 1	Clip after 1, 3, 5, 5, 3, and 1
Lap	**Queen**
Clip after 1, 3, 3, and 1	Clip after 1, 3, 5, 5, 5, 3, and 1
Twin	**King**
Clip after 1, 3, 3, 3, and 1	Clip after 1, 3, 5, 7, 7, 5, 3, and 1

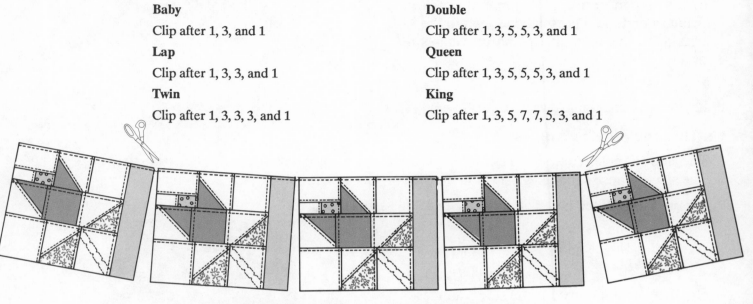

Example of a Baby Quilt - Clip apart into 1, 3, and 1

9. Sew multiple blocks into single diagonal rows. **Fingerpress both seams up at the cornerstone.**

10. Lay out your diagonal rows according to your quilt diagram found on pages 56 - 59.

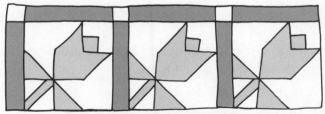

Example of a Three Block Row

Sewing the Remaining Lattice and Cornerstones

1. Stack the pieces in this order:

2. Assembly-line sew the remaining lattice and cornerstones.

3. **Sew the last cornerstone to the opposite end of a lattice.** Set aside for the single block in the bottom right corner.

4. Press the seams toward the lattice. Clip the threads.

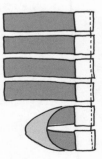

5. **Sew a single lattice/cornerstone to the right end of each diagonal row as indicated by the highlighted areas.**

6. **Sew the lattice with both cornerstones to the bottom right corner block as indicated by the lighter areas.** The remaining lattice/cornerstone pieces will be sewn to the triangles along the right and bottom edges of the quilt.

7. Press seams toward lattice.

8. Lay out the diagonal rows in order.

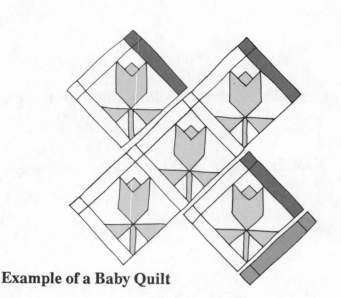

Example of a Baby Quilt

Cutting the Side Triangles

The side triangles come from cutting large squares on both diagonals into four triangles. The size of these squares is based on the size of your block.

If your Tulip Block is:	Then cut this size of square:
10 1/2" - 10 5/8"	18 1/4"
10 3/4" - 10 7/8"	18 1/2"
11"	18 3/4"

Cut this many squares for the side triangles:

Baby - 1		**Double - 3**	
Lap - 2		**Queen - 3**	
Twin - 2		**King - 4**	

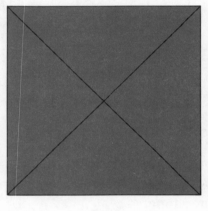

1. Fold and press diagonal folds in the large squares from corner to corner. Open.

2. Cut in fourths on the diagonals.

3. **Place a side triangle at the left end of each row and across the top of the quilt as indicated.** Smaller triangles will be placed at the corners.

Example of a Baby Quilt

# of Triangles for:

	Left Side	and	Top Edge
Baby -	1		1
Lap -	2		1
Twin -	3		1
Double -	3		2
Queen -	4		2
King -	4		3

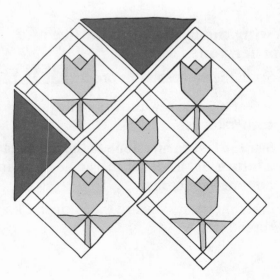

4. Flip each triangle right sides together to its row, **match the square bottom, and let the 3/8" tip of the triangle hang over at the top.** Pin the outside edges. Gently pat the triangle to fit. Pin the center.

5. Sew the triangles to the left end of each row, **with the triangle on the bottom.** Sew the triangles across the top to their rows.

6. Place each row back in the layout.

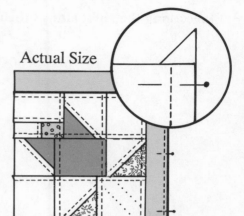

Actual Size

Completing the Triangles for the Bottom Edge

1. Stack the appropriate number of lattice/cornerstones and triangles **in this order:**

        Baby - 1

        Lap - 1

        Twin - 1

        Double - 2

        Queen - 2

        King - 3

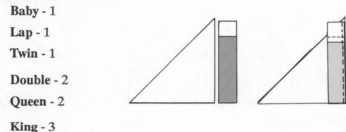

2. Flip the lattice right sides together to the triangle. **Match the square bottom, and let the 3/8" tip of the triangle extend at the top.** Pin and sew with the triangle on the bottom. Ease in the triangle if necessary.

3. Press the seam away from the triangle.

4. **Place in the empty spaces across the bottom of the quilt.**

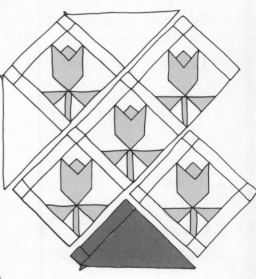

Completing the Triangles for the Right Side of the Quilt

1. Stack the appropriate number of lattice/cornerstones and triangles **in this order:**

        Baby - 1

        Lap - 2

        Twin - 3

        Double - 3

        Queen - 4

        King - 4

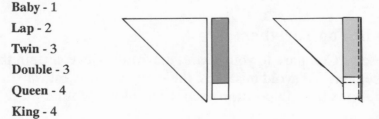

2. Flip the lattice right sides together to the triangle. Match the square top, and let the 3/8" tip of the triangle extend at the bottom. Pin and sew with the triangle on the bottom.

3. Place along the right side of the quilt.

Example of a Baby Quilt

Cutting the Corner Triangles

The four corner triangles come from cutting two squares on the diagonal. Regardless of the size of the quilt, only two squares are needed.

The size of the two squares is based on the size of your tulip block.

If your Tulip Block is:	Then cut this size of two squares:
10 1/2" - 10 5/8"	10 3/4"
10 3/4" - 10 7/8"	11"
11"	11 1/4"

1. Cut the squares in half on the diagonal.
2. Place at the four corners of the quilt layout.

Sewing the Rows of the Quilt Top Together

Examine your quilt rows closely. Compare to your layout diagram. Make certain that all pieces are in the proper placement. To avoid mistakes, the safest and easiest way to sew the quilt together is to lay the rows back in position each time before another piece is added.

The quilt is sewn together from the bottom right corner upward.

Sewing the Bottom Right Corner

1. Flip the side triangles right sides together to the block. Match and pin the square edges. Let the 3/8" tip hang over at the bottom. Sew with the triangle on the bottom.

2. Fold out and flat. Press the seams away from the light triangle.

3. Pin and sew on the corner triangle with the triangle on the bottom, and 3/8" tips hanging out equally on each end.

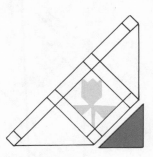

Example of All Quilt Sizes

Sewing the Next Diagonal Row to the Corner

Flip the three block diagonal row right sides together to the bottom right corner row. Match, pin, and sew.

The outside edges must line up. Allow only the 1/4" seam from the tip of the cornerstone to the edge of the top.

Example of Double, Queen, & King

Finishing the Top

Baby Quilt - See your layout. Sew on the single block row. Sew on the remaining corner triangles.

Lap and Twin - See your layout. Sew on the bottom left corner triangle, and the right side triangle.

Larger Quilts - See your layout. Sew the side triangles to the bottom and right of the diagonal row.

Example of King Only

1. Continue to sew from the bottom right upward, **sewing the rows together before adding the bottom and/or right side triangles.**

2. Sew on the remaining corner triangles.

3. Press the seams toward the lattice.

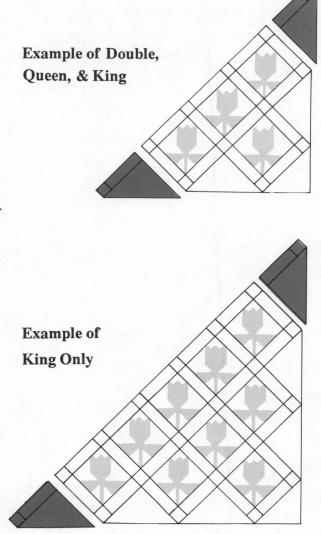

BABY QUILT

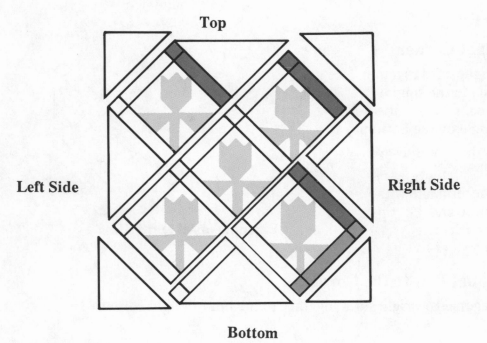

Top

Left Side

Right Side

Bottom

LAP QUILT

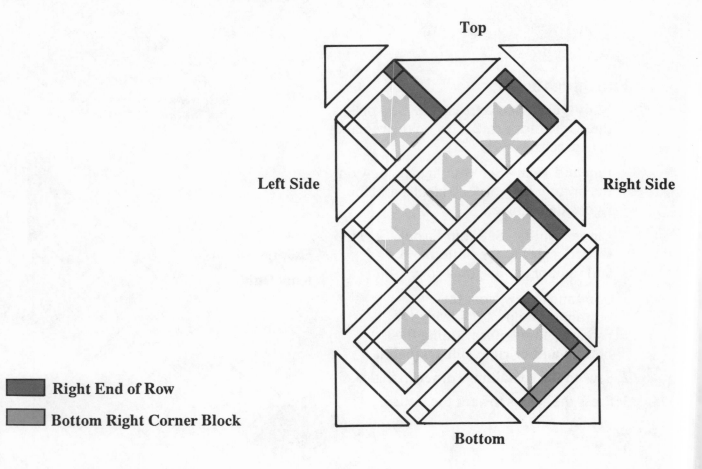

Top

Left Side

Right Side

Bottom

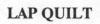 **Right End of Row**

Bottom Right Corner Block

TWIN SIZE QUILT

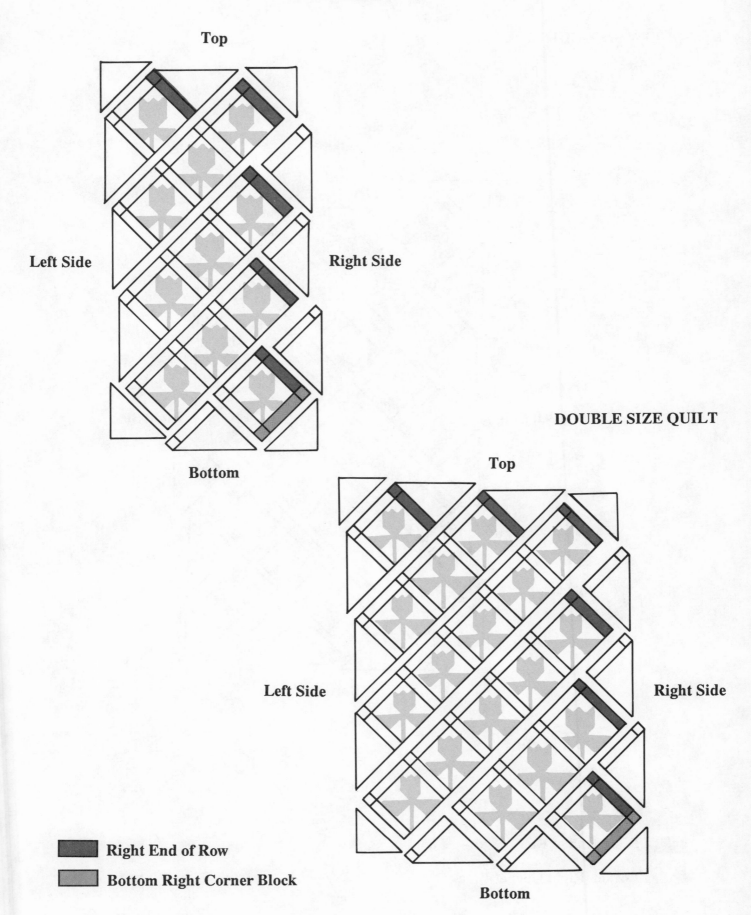

Top

Left Side

Right Side

Bottom

DOUBLE SIZE QUILT

Top

Left Side

Right Side

Bottom

Right End of Row

Bottom Right Corner Block

QUEEN SIZE QUILT

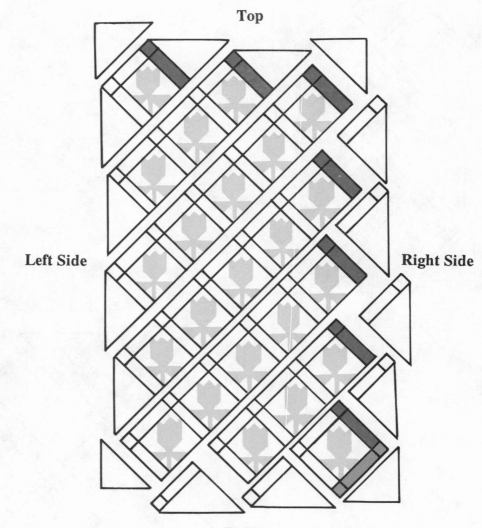

Top

Left Side

Right Side

Bottom

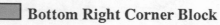 **Right End of Row**

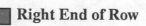 **Bottom Right Corner Block**

Top

Left Side

Right Side

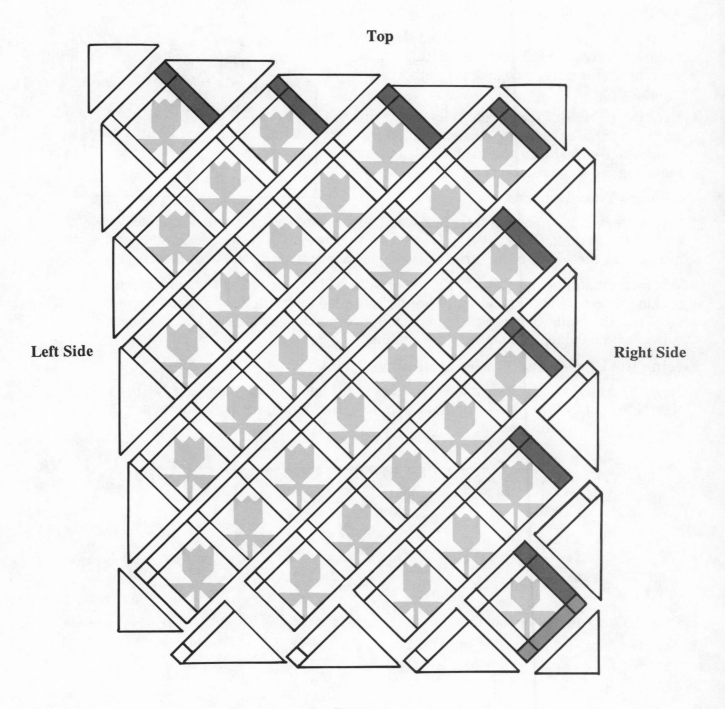

Bottom

Right End of Row

Bottom Right Corner Block

Borders and Backing for Your Tulip Quilt

Straightening the Outside Edges

It may be necessary to trim the outside edges even.

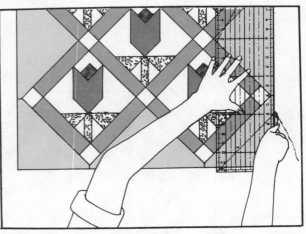

1. Lay it on a large table, and check which sides may need to be straightened. Slide the cutting mat along underneath the outside edge of the quilt when trimming.

2. Place the 1/4" line of the 6" x 24" ruler on the finished corner of the tulip block (or cornerstone). Sliver trim the side and corner triangles to **straighten without removing the seam allowance.**

Designing Your Borders

Be creative when adding borders. Suggested border yardage and border examples are given for each quilt. (Pages 10-21) However, you may wish to custom design the borders by changing the widths of the strips. This might change backing and batting yardage.

When custom fitting the quilt, lay the top on your bed before adding the borders and backing. Measure to find how much border is needed to get the fit you want. Keep in mind that the quilt will "shrink" approximately 3" in the length and width after tying, "stitching in the ditch," and/or machine quilting.

Piecing the Border and Optional Binding Strips

1. Seam the strips of each fabric into long pieces by assembly-line sewing. Lay the first strip right side up. Lay the second strip right sides to it. Backstitch, stitch the short ends together, and backstitch again.

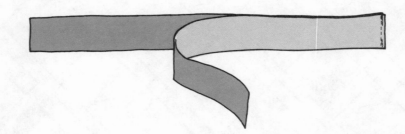

2. Take the strip on the top and fold it so the right side is up.

3. Place the third strip right sides to it, backstitch, stitch, and backstitch again.

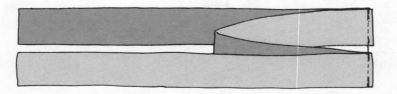

4. Continue assembly-line sewing all the short ends together into long pieces for each fabric.

5. Clip the threads holding the strips together.

Sewing the Borders to the Tulip Quilt Top

1. Measure down the center to find the length.

2. Cut two strips that measurement from the First Border fabric. Square off each end with the rotary cutter and ruler as you cut.

3. Pin in the center and then to each side, easing or stretching as needed. Sew. Fold out and flat. Press away from the quilt top.

4. Measure across the center to find the width, including the first borders.

5. Cut two strips that measurement. Square off the ends as you cut.

6. Pin to top and bottom, easing or stretching as needed. Sew. Fold out and flat. All borders are added in this manner.

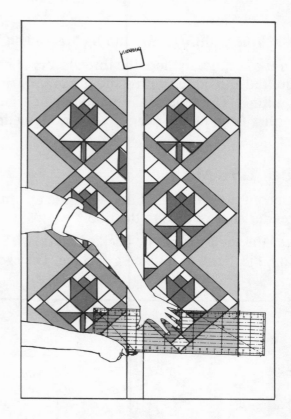

Preparing the Backing from 45" Wide Fabric

1. Following your Cutting Chart, fold the long backing crosswise and cut into equal pieces. If you custom fitted your quilt, you may need to adjust these measurements. If your backing is too narrow, use your leftover fabrics, and add a section down the middle. If your backing is too short, add a strip to each end from leftovers.

2. Tear off the selvages and seam the backing pieces together.

3. Embroider your name and date on the backing with hand stitching or machine writing. Consider adding your state as many quilts travel across the country.

Piecing the Bonded Batting

1. If the batting needs to be pieced to get the desired size, cut and butt the two straight edges closely without overlapping.

2. Whipstitch the edges together with a double strand of thread. Do not pull the threads tightly as this will create a hard ridge visible on the outside of the quilt.

Two Different Methods of Finishing

1. Quick Turn Method

The first method, the Quick Turn, is the easier and faster way of finishing the quilt. Thick batting is "rolled" into the middle of the quilt, and the layers are held together with ties. Borders may be "stitched in the ditch" for additional dimension.

2. Machine Quilting and Binding Method on Page 66

In the second method, the three layers of backing, batting, and quilt top are machine quilted and bound with a straight grain strip of binding. A thin batting is used for ease in quilting. The solid squares and/or side triangles may be "free motion" machine quilted with a Tulip motif. (Page 71.) If quilting design is selected, mark fabric before layering.

Quick Turn Method

1. Lay out the backing fabric, right side up, on a large table or floor. Clamp to the table with binder clips or tape to the floor.

2. Lay the quilt top on the backing fabric with right sides together. Stretch and smooth the top. Pin. Trim away excess backing. They should be the same size.

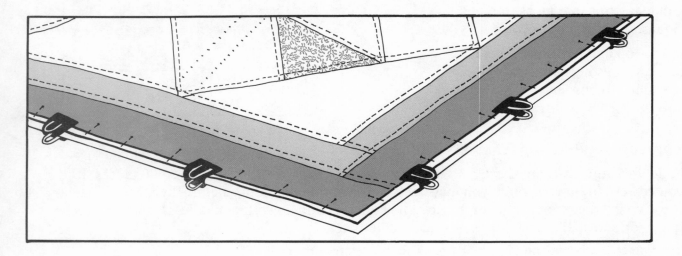

3. Stitch around the four sides of the quilt, leaving a 24" opening in the middle of one long side. Do not turn the quilt right side out.

4. Lay the quilt on top of the batting. Smooth and trim the batting to the same size as the quilt top.

5. To assure that the batting stays out to the edges, whipstitch the batting to the 1/4" seam allowance around the outside edge of the quilt.

Turning the Quilt Top

This part of making your quilt is particularly exciting. One person can turn the quilt alone, but it's fun to turn it into a 10-minute family or neighborhood event with three or four others. **Read this whole section before beginning.**

1. If you are working with a group, station the people at the corners of the quilt. If working alone, start in one corner opposite the opening.

2. Roll the corners and sides tightly to keep the batting in place as you roll toward the opening.

If several people are helping, all should roll toward the opening. If only one is doing the rolling, use a knee to hold down one corner while stretching over to the other corners.

3. Open up the opening over this huge wad of fabric and batting, and pop the quilt right side out through the hole.

4. Unroll carefully with the layers together.

5. Lay the quilt flat on the floor or on a very large table. Work out all wrinkles and bumps by stationing two people opposite each other around the quilt. Have each person grasp the edge and tug the quilt in opposite directions.

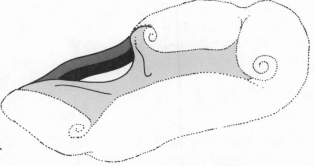

6. You can also relocate any batting by reaching inside the quilt through the opening with a yardstick. Hold the edges and shake the batting into place if necessary.

7. Slipstitch the opening shut.

Finishing the Quick Turn Quilt

You may choose to tie your entire quilt, or machine quilt by "stitching in the ditch" around the borders and tying in the block corner. (This would apply to both settings.)

A thick batting is difficult to machine quilt except for the borders, as it is hard to get all the rolled thickness to fit through the keyhole of the sewing machine.

Tying the Quilt

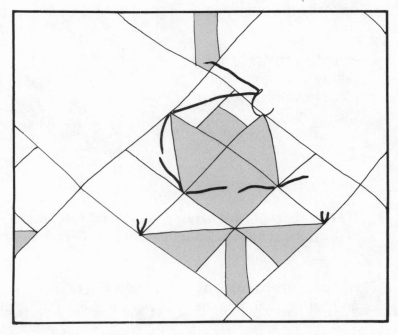

1. Thread a large-eyed curved needle with six strands of embroidery floss, crochet thread, or other thread of your choice.

2. Plan where you want your ties placed. You may want to outline the tulip with ties, or just tie the outside corners of the solid squares or cornerstones.

   Do not tie in the borders if you wish to "stitch in the ditch."

3. Starting in the center of the quilt and working to the outside, take a 1/4" stitch through all thicknesses at the points you wish to tie. Draw the curved needle along to each point, going in and out, and replacing the tying material as needed.

4. Clip all the stitches midway.

5. Tie the strands into surgeon's square knots by taking the strand on the right and wrapping it twice. Pull the knot tight. Take the strand on the left, wrap it twice, and pull the knot tight.

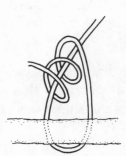

Right over left and wrap twice.

Left over right and wrap twice.

6. Clip the strands so they are 1/2" to 1" long.

Stitching in the Ditch

For more dimensional borders, you may choose to "stitch in the ditch" rather than tie the borders. A walking foot or even-feed foot sewing machine attachment is necessary to keep the three layers feeding at the same rate.

1. Change your stitch length to 10 stitches per inch. Match your bobbin color of thread to your backing color. Loosen the top tension and thread with the soft nylon invisible thread.

2. Safety pin the length of the borders.

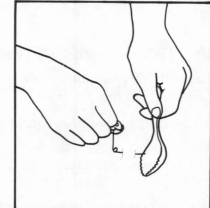

Quick and Easy Safety Pinning with a Grapefruit Spoon

Grasp the opened pin in your right hand and the grapefruit spoon in your left hand. Push the pin through the three layers, and bring the tip of the pin back out. Just as the tip of the pin surfaces, catch the tip in the serrated edge of the spoon, twist the side of the spoon up while pushing down on the pin, to close it.

3. Place the needle in the depth of the seam. Lock your threads with 1/8" of tiny stitches when you begin and end your sewing. Run your hand underneath to feel for puckers. Grasp the quilt with your left hand above the sewing machine, and grasp the quilt ten inches below the walking foot with your right hand as you stitch. If you need to ease in the top fabric, feed the quilt through the machine by pushing the layers of fabric and batting forward underneath the walking foot. If puckering occurs, remove your stitches and resew.

4. Remove safety pins and store in opened position.

Machine Quilting and Binding Method

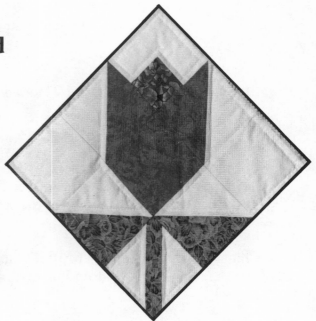

The easiest method of machine quilting is "stitching in the ditch" in the diagonal seams with a walking foot, using thin batting.

A more advanced method is marking the tulip design on the corners and side triangles and free motion quilting them with the use of a darning foot. You have freedom to stitch forward, backwards, and to the sides without the use of your presser foot or feed dogs. However, this method requires practice.

You could also "outline quilt" 1/4" away from the outside edges of the tulip, and the side triangles. Use the edge of your walking foot as your guide.

Marking Tulip Designs for Free Motion Quilting with Darning Foot

If you wish to free motion quilt, trace the tulip design onto the quilt before layering with batting and backing.

1. Photocopy the tulip design found on page 71.
2. Tape the tulip design to the top of a light table. You can make your own light table quite simply by opening the leaves on a dining table, placing a large piece of glass on the top of the table opening and placing a table lamp underneath the glass.
3. Lay the quilt on top. Center each side triangle over the design and, with the quilt marking pencil, trace the design. Repeat this procedure with the corner triangles.

Adding the Backing and Batting

1. Stretch out the backing right side down on a large floor area or table. Tape down on a floor area or clamp onto a table with large binder clips.
2. Place and smooth out the batting on top. Lay the quilt top right side up and centered on top of the batting. Completely smooth and stretch all layers until they are flat. Tape or clip securely. The backing and batting should extend at least 2" on all sides.

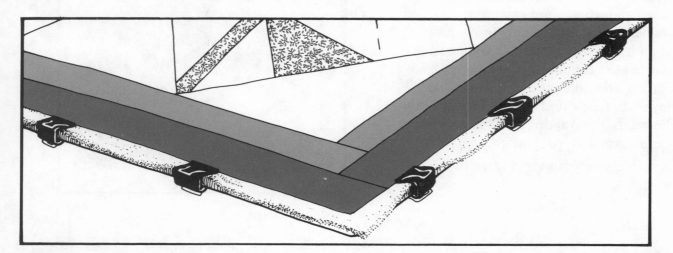

3. Place safety pins throughout the quilt away from lines where you will be machine stitching. Begin pinning in the center and work to the outside. They should be spaced every 5". See page 65.

4. Trim the backing and batting to within 2" of the outside edge of the quilt.

5. Roll the quilt tightly from the outside edge in toward the middle squares. Hold this roll with metal bicycle clips or pins.

6. Slide this roll into the keyhole of the sewing machine.

7. "Stitch in the ditch." See page 65.

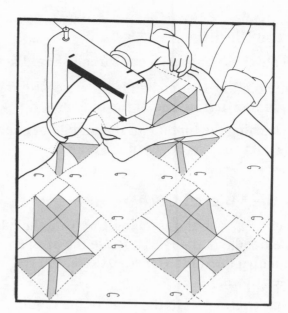

Free Motion Machine Quilting Technique

Refer to your instruction manual for directions on how to darn with your machine. You will need to use a darning foot, and drop the feed dogs or cover them with a plate. Practice before attempting the free hand quilting.

No stitch length is required as you control the length stitch. Lower the speed of your machine if available. Use a fine needle and a little hole throat plate.

Use invisible thread in the top. Match the bobbin thread to the backing.

1. Roll the quilt to one corner and hold in place with bicycle clips.

2. Bring the bobbin thread up at the beginning point. Lower the needle into the quilt and drop the foot. The quilt should move freely under the darning foot. Move the fabric very slowly and take a few tiny stitches to lock them. Snip off the tails of the threads.

3. With your eyes watching the line ahead of the needle, and your fingertips stretching the fabric and acting as a quilting hoop, move the fabric in a steady motion while the machine is running at a constant speed. Do not move the fabric fast as this will break the needle. Keep the top of the block in the same position by moving the fabric underneath the needle side to side, and forward and backward.

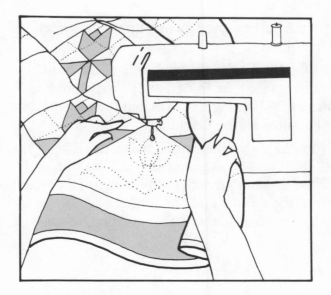

4. Lock off with tiny stitches and clip the threads.

5. Do not trim backing and batting.

Adding the Binding

Use 10 stitches per inch. Your thread should match your binding. Use a walking foot.

1. Press the binding strip in half lengthwise with right sides out. Turn under a 1/2" hem on the beginning narrow end of the binding strip.

2. Begin stitching the binding to the middle of one long side. Line up the raw edges of the binding with the raw edges of the quilt.

Making the Mitered Corner

1. At the corner, stop the stitching 1/4" from the edge with the needle in the fabric. Raise the presser foot and turn the quilt to the next side. Put the foot back down.

2. Stitch backwards 1/4" to the edge of the binding, raise the presser foot, and pull the quilt forward slightly. *Step 1*

3. Fold the binding strip straight up on the diagonal. Fingerpress in the diagonal fold. *Step 2*

4. Fold the binding strip straight down with the diagonal fold underneath. Line up the top of the fold with the raw edge of the binding underneath.

5. Begin sewing 1/4" in from the edge at the original pivot point. *Step 3*

6. Continue stitching and mitering the corners around the outside of the quilt.

7. End the binding by overlapping the end strip approximately 1" at the beginning point. Trim off any excess binding.

8. Trim the batting and backing up to the raw edges of the binding.

9. Fold the binding to the back side of the quilt. Pin in place so that the folded edge on the binding covers the stitching line. Tuck in the excess fabric at the miter on the diagonal.

10. From the right side, "stitch in the ditch" using invisible thread on the right side of the quilt, and a bobbin thread to match the binding on the wrong side of the quilt. Catch the folded edge of the binding on the backside with the stitching. *Step 4*

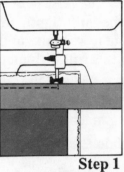

Step 1

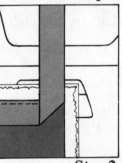

Step 2

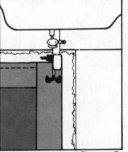

Step 3

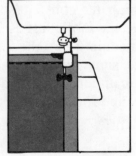

Step 4

Making the Pillow

See detailed instructions for making the tulip block.

1. Sew the tip patch. Square to 4". See pages 26 and 27.

2. Make two dark petal patches and two green leaf patches. See page 33.

3. Sew the stem to the 4" light square. See page 34.

4. Sew the block together. See pages 38-40.

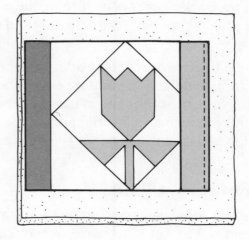

5. Pin corner triangles to opposite sides of the block, allowing a 3/8" tip to extend on each side. Sew with the triangles on the bottom. Fold out, and press seams toward the triangles. Add the two remaining corner triangles, and press. Straighten the outside edges.

6. Center the block on the batting, and "stitch in the ditch" around the tulip. See page 65.

7. Pin 2 1/2" borders to two opposite sides. Trim even with the block. Stitch through all thicknesses. Fold out flat.

8. Pin, trim, and stitch on the two remaining borders. Fold out flat. Trim the batting.

9. Place the pre-gathered lace right sides together to the middle of one side. Fold the end back 1". Pin around the outside edge, easing in additional lace at the corners, and stitch.

10. Cut the backing the same size as the pillow front. Pin the two right sides together with the lace enclosed in the middle.

11. Stitch around the outside edge, leaving a 6" opening in the middle of one side. Turn.

12. Stuff firmly. Slipstitch the opening shut.

Making the Two Shams

1. Count out (5) 6" ruffle strips for each sham. Continuously stitch the short ends together into two long circular pieces.

2. With right sides out, fold and press each long strip in half lengthwise.

3. Set the machine with a wide zigzag and long stitch.

4. Lay the cord 1/8" from the raw edges. Zigzag over the cord being careful not to catch it.

5. Draw up the cord to fit the ruffle to the sham top. Using the seams in the ruffle as your guide, draw up one strip length for each narrow side, and 1 1/2 strip lengths for each long side. Space the gathers evenly as you pin in place.

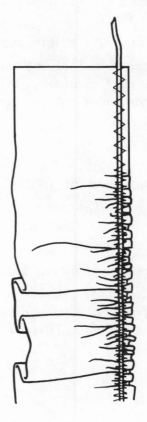

6. Stitch around the outside edge, including the zigzag stitching in the seam allowance. Remove only the cord that shows on the right side.

7. Hem the backing pieces by turning the raw edge under 1" on one long side only and stitching.

8. Lay one backing piece right sides together to the front, matching the outside edges and placing the hem near the center. Lay the second backing piece on top, overlapping in the center. Pin and stitch all around the outside edge.

9. Turn right side out.

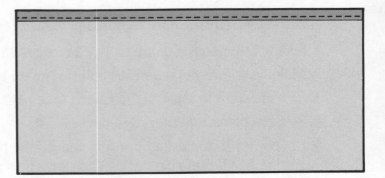

Making the Dust Ruffle

1. Remove the selvages on the "no show" lining and piece together lengthwise. When placed on the mattress, this seam runs side to side.

2. Remove the mattress, and place the lining on top.

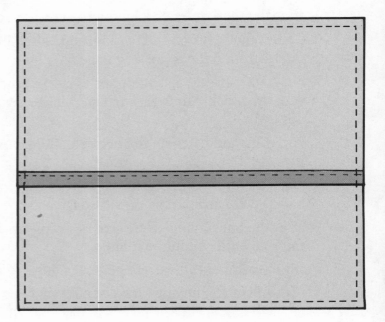

3. Trim to fit, allowing an extra 1/2" on all sides for the seam allowance. Round the corners.

4. Hem the end at the head of the bed.

5. Divide the sides and foot into eight equal parts and mark with pins.

6. Sew the short ends of the ruffle strips together.

7. Hem one short end and the bottom edge with a 1/4" rolled hem. *If available, use the rolled hem foot attachment on your sewing machine.*

8. Fold the ruffle fabric into eight equal parts, and mark with pins.

9. Gather the ruffle to fit the "no show" lining on the two long sides and foot of the bed.

Use the string method of gathering as described on the pillow ruffle, a ruffler attachment, or a gathering foot attachment.

10. Trim the excess ruffle fabric, and hem.

If the bed has a footboard, work on the three sides separately with hemmed sides at each corner so that the ruffle will fit over the bed frame.

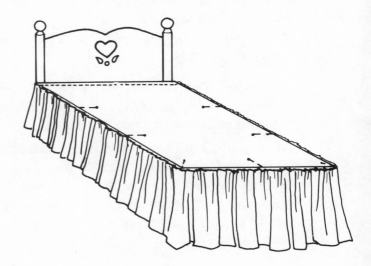

Free Motion Tulip Design

Follow the directions on page 67 for setting up your machine.

Trace following the solid lines.

The sewing direction to follow when free motion quilting is represented by the arrowed lines.

Drop your needle into the fabric at the tip of tulip and pull up the bobbin thread (1). Free motion down the tip and swing to the left petal (2), down to the left leaf (3), to the right leaf (4), up to the right petal (5), and up to the starting point (6).

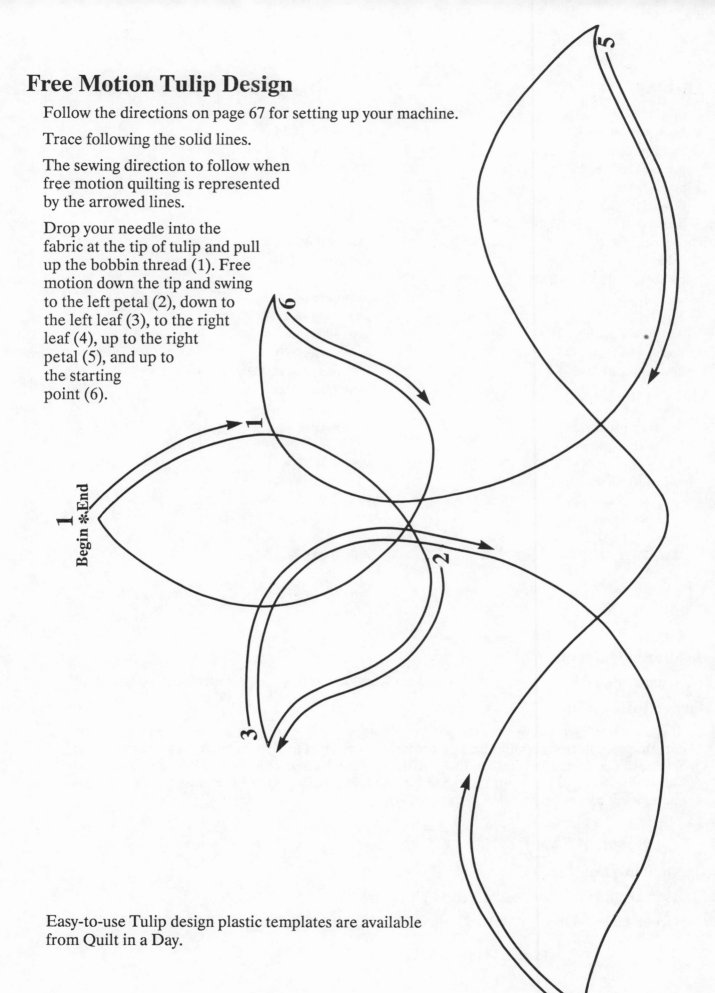

Easy-to-use Tulip design plastic templates are available from Quilt in a Day.

71

Index

Acknowledgement

A grateful thank you to all the quiltmakers who loaned their tulip quilts for photographing.

Order Information

If you do not have a fine quilt shop in your area, you may write for a complete catalog and current price list of all books and patterns published by Quilt in a Day®. If you are ever in Southern California, North San Diego County, drop by and visit the Quilt in a Day Center. Our quilt shop and classroom is located in the La Costa Meadows Business Center. Write ahead for a current class schedule and map.

Quilt in a Day®

Quilt in a Day, Inc.

1955 Diamond Street, San Marcos, California 92069

Order Line: 1-800-U2 KWILT (1-800-825-9458)   Information Line: 1-619-591-0081